"It is not if, but rather when we will each need time to Rest so we may heal. *The Art and Law of Rest* is a much needed and superbly crafted guide on navigating the all-too-bewildering landscape of employment and income protections we have access to though rarely realize or utilize. I have both personally and professionally witnessed the unintended consequences of working while mentally compromised, unaware that an alternative exists. Andy Chu, Esq. is like a Jedi master, patiently teaching us how to recognize the need for Rest and how to access and advocate for the supports at our fingertips. His expertise, authenticity, and empathy fuel every word. This is essential reading for every professional care provider, HR specialist, and loving member of society."
   — Dawn Gross, MD, PhD, Hospice and Palliative Medicine, UCSF; Medical Director, ANX Hospice; Founder/CEO, Dyalogues, PBC

"Empathetic but full of expertise, the book is thorough and informative regarding what people's rights are, sharing advice for navigating systems that can seem confusing, indifferent, and even hostile."
   — *Foreword Reviews*

"This is a book with a real mission and valuable information. Andy Chu is an expert in the field of paid medical leave and disability income. Anyone considering these topics should start with this book."
   — Michael Bernick, former Director of Employment Development Department of CA

"Chu is particularly effective at explaining the differences among benefits programs, how to communicate with health care providers, and how to transition from short- to long-term disability, eschewing complicated verbiage for clear-cut, witty counsel."
   — *Kirkus Reviews*

"I often say the folks who are least able to deal with the system are the ones who have to deal with it the most. When you are sick or disabled it is especially tough to navigate these systems. Andy's book helps to level the playing field so that everyone can understand what their rights are. His writing is as lovely, clear, and accessible as he is. Andy's career has been all about public service. This book reflects that commitment."
— Bill Hirsh, Esq., Executive Director of AIDS Legal Referral Panel

"With more than 20 years of legal and practical experience the expert author has written masterfully, accessibly, and coherently about disability. The reader will emerge with a complete understanding about the processing and advocacy needed to establish disability. The book permits the reader to tailor the knowledge so that it applies to the individual needs."
— G. Andrew H. Benjamin, JD, PhD, ABPP, Clinical Professor of Psychology & Affiliate Professor of Law, University of Washington

The Art and Law of *Rest*

A Legal Guide to Paid Medical Leave for Mental Health

ANDY CHU, ESQ.

The Art and Law of Rest:
A Legal Guide to Paid Medical Leave for Mental Health
© 2023, Andy Chu, Esq. All rights reserved.

Published by Nimsa Press, San Francisco, California

ISBN 979-8-9869908-0-4 (paperback)
ISBN 979-8-9869908-1-1 (eBook)
Library of Congress Control Number: 2022922071

Without limiting the rights under copyright reserved above, no part of this publication may be reproduced, stored in or introduced into a retrieval system, or transmitted in any form or by any means (electronic, mechanical, photocopying, recording or otherwise whether now or hereafter known), without the prior written permission of both the copyright owner and the above publisher of this book, except by a reviewer who wishes to quote brief passages in connection with a review written for insertion in a magazine, newspaper, broadcast, website, blog or other outlet in conformity with United States and International Fair Use or comparable guidelines to such copyright exceptions.

This book is intended to provide accurate information with regard to its subject matter and reflects the opinion and perspective of the author. However, in times of rapid change, ensuring all information provided is entirely accurate and up-to-date at all times is not always possible. Therefore, the author and publisher accept no responsibility for inaccuracies or omissions and specifically disclaim any liability, loss or risk, personal, professional or otherwise, which may be incurred as a consequence, directly or indirectly, of the use and/or application of any of the contents of this book.

This book is dedicated to all the workers in the US who sometimes need to rest and heal.

Edye,

Thank you for your support + friendship.
May you always be surrounded by Love + Good Health.

Andy Chen
S.F. 10/2023

Contents

Preface 1
- Disclaimer 9
- Standard Terms 9

Part One 11

1 The Infamous "Can I" Questions 13
- How Much Do You Want to Suffer? 15
- To Prevent a Disability Crisis, Take a Paid Medical Leave 17
- Midas, a Karōshi Victim 18
- A New Midas 20

2 A Model Definition of Mental Disability 23
- Illness 24
- Jim's Story 29
- Loss of Income 31
- Effect on Work 32

3 Telling Your Story 39
- Susan's Story 42
- To Your Doctor: Symptoms and Limitations 46

- To Your Insurer: The Function Report 54

Part Two 63

4 **Getting to Know Your Maps**...65
- Short-Term Disability: Introduction/Lily's Story 67
- Short-Term Disability: State Disability 68
- Short-Term Disability: Employer Sponsored Short-Term Disability Insurance (STDI)................................71
- Long-Term Disability: Introduction 76
- Long-Term Disability: Long-Term Disability Insurance (LTDI)...77
- Long-Term Disability: Social Security Disability Insurance (SSDI)...79
- Han's Story...85
- Job and Health Insurance Protections......................88

5 **Seven Steps to Your Paid Medical Leave: Introduction**........93
- Step One: Start Your Healing Journey with a Supportive Doctor 95
- Step Two: Get to Know Your Protections...................98
- Step Three: Decide on a Date Last Work (DLW) 102
- Step Four: Apply for Job and Health Insurance Protections 102
- Step Five: Apply for Disability Benefits....................103
- Step Six: Rest, Heal, and Maintain Your Benefits 106
- Step Seven: Consider Your Future 107

6 Epilogue 115
7 Glossary 119
8 Acknowledgments 125
9 About Me..127

Preface

A few years ago, my aunt became disabled. I helped her, naturally.

"I had no idea you knew so much about disability income," she said to me during one of my visits to her in the hospital. She only knew I did some kind of public interest law.

I asked her why she didn't apply for disability earlier and go on a paid medical leave. She could have killed herself from overwork.

"I was worried about money. I didn't know I could get disability income during a medical leave. And I wanted to work, Andy. I didn't want to be disabled. I have worked my whole life. I was scared. All the information about disability was so confusing. I didn't know where to start."

I told her a story that I sometimes tell my clients.

> Imagine it is springtime, and you have been invited to a party in a rural town called Bountiful. It is so secluded and far away, the map on your iPhone won't get you there.

You go online and find a map of Bountiful from the federal government. But it only contains the federal highways.

You are disappointed, because you know you could use the state roads too. But those are on a separate state map.

Then a friend tells you about the pretty little country roads within the county line, but you can only find them on the county map.

You see the task in front of you and frown: get the maps, scale them, put them together and locate the intersections. You don't want to do this. You call the host for help, and you are told, "Oh, but that's how everybody does it!"

"And that's how everybody does it when it comes to applying for disability income," I said. "Think of the federal highway as Social Security benefits, the state road as State Disability benefits, and the county road as commercial disability insurance."

I beamed, satisfied with my own explanation.

"Jeez. How are we supposed to figure these things out, especially when we're sick?"

I pointed to my head, "All the roads are here. I can tell you where to go and how to get there."

"You are such a show-off, Andy."

We laughed.

She asked what I had been doing all these years. Generations of family drama had separated us.

"I work at a nonprofit. We help low-income folks get disability benefits when they have physical or mental problems."

"So, what about people who are not low income—like me? How would I get help if you were not my nephew?"

I didn't say anything. The truth was that most American workers find little help, if any.

Silently, she looked away. She whispered that her company didn't help her. They even tried to get rid of her. She felt betrayed, especially by her friend who worked in the human resources department.

"Your company isn't doing anything new. It's not personal." I spoke in Cantonese, our native tongue.

"They are heartless."

At the time, I agreed with her. Now that I am older, I see things differently. The individual is not heartless, but society demands productivity and discourages humaneness. Trapped inside the society, we—like Ionesco's rhinos—have lost touch with our humanity.

The Idea of a Book

That night, I strolled along Portola Drive overlooking San Francisco's downtown, thinking about my aunt. I wished there were some way to cheer her up. My brother told me once about how much this aunt loved self-help books. A guidebook on disability would be perfect for her.

On my way to the bookstore, I imagined the perfect guidebook. It would explain when and why workers should take a paid medical leave and how to replace their lost wages with disability income. It would explain the different types of disability income, when to apply for them, and how. It would unite the different maps of my

Bountiful story. It would explain job and health insurance protections as well. It would dispel the many myths about disability that have ruined lives. It would help workers avoid common mistakes. It would teach them self-advocacy skills, the same ones that disability attorneys like me teach our clients.

As a disability attorney, I had never thought of buying such a book, just as I had grown up in New York City and never bothered going to the Statue of Liberty. My visit to the bookstore was a surprise. There weren't many guidebooks on disability, even though there were more than 8 million US workers on Social Security disability benefits, not including all the disabled workers on other types of disability benefits. Those eight million also didn't include people whose claims were denied. I did not find one book that provided an integrated overview of the federal, state, and commercial disability benefits.

I couldn't buy a book that didn't exist, so I sent my aunt flowers instead. Turns out she was allergic. But I made up for it—I got her disability income. For many years, every time she thanked me for helping her, I would think about that nonexistent guidebook.

• • •

In 2019, I took a break from my fifteen years of service as a public interest attorney. With newfound freedom, I began to write this book to help workers take paid medical leave and access disability income. It is written for folks whose income is too high to receive free legal and social services, but also not high enough to live without worrying about income; folks who have worked for many years if not most of their lives; and folks who are suddenly upended by disability. In other words, folks like my aunt.

PREFACE

When workers like my aunt need an extended break from work, they often do so without guidance. Their income level does not qualify them for free social services. They have worked for a long time and "paid into the system," so they have decent disability protections. However, they don't know how to use their benefits and where to start. This book is the place to start.

This book shows you how to take a paid medical leave. A paid medical leave is when you take a medical leave from work but still get paid. The payments come from disability insurance to replace lost wages. A big part of this book is on how to win your disability claim so that you get paid during your leave. While you may not have to apply for disability income for your medical leave, you should. Otherwise, your medical leave will likely be *unpaid*. Many workers unwittingly go on unpaid leave when they should get paid medical leave instead. Don't let that happen to you. (An exception exists for workers in states with Paid Family Medical Leave [PFML], which will be discussed in this book as well.)

On the flip side, you can apply for disability without a medical leave. Some ill workers skip the medical leave and resign. They don't need the job protections of a medical leave because they expect Long-Term Disability. They want to secure their financial future with disability income. If that's you, focus on the parts of the book on disability income and skim through the job protection sections. Having said that, keep in mind that employment status comes with many protections. If you must resign, do so only after deliberation. Generally, a paid medical leave is the safest transition between full employment and Long-Term Disability.

This book will make you a well-informed worker and consumer, not an expert. It provides a panoramic view of the disability landscape without any deep (and difficult) analysis. I try to avoid mathematical calculations. The information is general; exceptions may apply to your situation. Not every worker is eligible for every benefit and protection discussed in this book.

This book is focused on mental health for several reasons. First, mental illness is one of the leading causes of disability. It is the second most common reason for Social Security disability, right behind skeletomuscular diseases.

Second, mental health disability is not as clear cut as physical disability. Many people don't even know they are suffering until they are in crisis—losing their job, income and health insurance (one after another or all at once). This book is written to help people recognize mental health disabilities early and avert that crisis.

Third, mental health disability is riddled with myths and misconceptions that have ruined lives. Many people do not apply for benefits simply because they lack information, or worse, are misinformed. This book dispels the falsehoods one by one. I hope the truth will empower people to use their disability benefits, take time off and take care of their mental health.

Outline of the Book

Part One contains the following chapters:

- **Chapter 1:** The Infamous "Can I" Questions; How Much Do You Want to Suffer?; To Prevent a Disability Crisis, Take a Paid Medical Leave; Midas, a Karōshi Victim; A New Midas
- **Chapter 2:** A Model Definition of Mental Disability; Mental Illness; Jim's Story; Loss of Income; Effect on Work
- **Chapter 3:** Telling Your Story; Susan's Story; To Your Doctor: Symptoms and Limitations; To Your Insurer: The Function Report

PREFACE

This section of the book is for people who are unsure about medical leave and disability income. In Chapter 1, I explain what disability income is and is not, and how it protects workers during a medical leave. I discuss why people don't take a paid medical leave when they should, and how to avoid a disability crisis. In Chapter 2, readers will learn a model definition of mental health disability, an easy tool to help determine whether they should consider disability. In Chapter 3, readers will learn how to document and communicate pain and suffering in a way that *supports,* not derails, disability claims.

If you have already decided to go on a paid medical leave and just want to learn how, you may wish to read Part Two before Part One. However, both are equally important if you want a proper understanding of paid medical leave and disability protections.

Part Two contains the following chapters:

- **Chapter 4:** Getting to Know Your Maps; Short-Term Disability: Introduction/Lily's Story; Short-Term Disability: State Disability; Short-Term Disability: Employer Sponsored Short-Term Disability Insurance (STDI); Long-Term Disability: Introduction; Long-Term Disability: Long-Term Disability Insurance (LTDI); Long-Term Disability: Social Security Disability Insurance (SSDI); Han's Story; Job and Health Insurance Protections
- **Chapter 5:** Seven Steps to Your Paid Medical Leave: Introduction; Step One: Start Your Healing Journey with A Supportive Doctor; Step Two: Get to Know Your Protections; Step Three: Decide on a Date Last Work (DLW); Step Four: Apply for Job and Health Insurance Protections; Step

Five: Apply for Disability Benefits; Step Six: Rest, Heal and Maintain Your Benefits; Step Seven: Consider Your Future

This section is where the rubber meets the road. You will start by learning the different roads (types of income benefits), and when and how to use them. Then you will learn how to secure your job and health insurance for your paid medical leave. In Chapter 5, the final chapter, I integrate the previous four chapters into a roadmap, a step-by-step guide on how to take a paid medical leave.

• • •

While this book helps people get the income they need to survive, survival is not enough, not for human beings. We must have meaning. Disabling illness can be a blessing in disguise, as I have seen in so many of my clients. They find new meaning in life. Some get education in a new field that they have always wanted to try. One client became a chef, and the State of California paid for his cooking classes as part of his vocational rehab. Another client became a florist; working with plants was her childhood dream.

Some clients reevaluate their relationships and reconnect with loved ones. One young gay man, who became homeless and estranged from his family due to his sexuality, moved home after he was awarded Social Security disability benefits. His parents drove three hours from the wine country to my office to pick him up. When they saw how wasted their son had become, they hugged him, cried and asked for his forgiveness.

You too can view disabling illness as a road to find meaning and purpose. What do you want to do with your life? Who do you love? What haven't you done that you regret most? *Who are you?* Perhaps in your busy life, you haven't had the chance to consider any of this recently. Like it or not, now is your chance. Be brave.

It takes guts to declare: I have a serious illness. I need a medical leave. I am going to apply for benefits. I am going to put my finances in order. I am going to rest and heal. I am going to reconnect with the people and things I love the most.

You can do this haphazardly and let your illness take you wherever it leads. Most of my clients did. They had one crisis after another. But you don't have to. You can live wisely with your illness by planning ahead and making smart choices—that's the *art of rest:* knowing when to take a break and what legal protections to use.

Disclaimer

While I am a licensed attorney, reading this book doesn't establish an attorney-client relationship between us. If you need an attorney, a good place to start is by contacting your local state bar.

The information in this book is general in nature. Exceptions may exist, as well as exceptions to the exceptions! Not everything in this book will apply to your specific situation. This book is no substitute for the advice of a competent attorney in your jurisdiction.

There is no guarantee that you will win your disability claims by following the advice of this book. No one can guarantee that.

I am not an accountant or tax lawyer. Receiving disability income has tax consequences. Please consult your tax adviser.

Governmental benefit amounts slightly change every year. This book uses numbers from 2022 and 2023. For the latest numbers, visit www.andychulaw.com/book.

Standard Terms

The disability insurance world is fragmented. Different disability benefits may use the same word to mean different things, or use different words to mean the same thing. To achieve a coherent, integrated view of the disability systems, I have standardized certain terms. If you see a word or a phrase capitalized and you don't know why, it is probably a standard term. Standard terms are defined in the glossary.

CHAPTER 1

The Infamous "Can I" Questions

When you are very ill, it is natural to ask yourself, *can I still work?*

This question has ruined many lives.

Other devastating "Can I" questions include: Can I make it to the office? Can I work through the pain? Can I just work slower (at half the pace)? Hardworking but misinformed, some believe that as long as they *can* work, despite their suffering, they are not disabled, don't qualify for disability benefits, and don't deserve a break. They think only people in wheelchairs or psychiatric wards should benefit from disability protections. They continue to work until they have become completely debilitated, meeting their own strict definition of disability. I imagine Daniel was one of these people.

Daniel was sick and couldn't work, but he kept working anyway. His employer demoted him. He kept working. Finally, his employer forced him to resign. After leaving the employer, Daniel applied for disability benefits under the employer's disability insurance policy. The insurance company denied his claim.

The insurance company reasoned that since Daniel had kept working even while he was ill, he couldn't have been *that* disabled so his disability must have begun after he left the employer, when he was no longer insured under the employer's policy. Daniel sued.

The court disagreed with the insurance company. It noted that people often work despite their disability because they can't afford to lose income and health insurance. Just because Daniel kept working didn't mean he was not disabled. The court granted Daniel relief a year before he died.

His full name was Daniel Rochow; his case was *Rochow v. Life Insurance Company of North America (2007)*. When I first read this case, I felt sad for Daniel because he had spent the last years of his life fighting the insurance company. If Daniel had applied for disability while he was still employed, there would have been no doubt that he was covered under the employer's disability insurance policy.

So why didn't Daniel apply while he was still employed? Why did he not apply when it was most advantageous? Probably because he had asked himself the wrong questions, those "Can I" questions. He kept answering, "Yes, I can," "I can make it to the office, even though I should be in bed," "I can work through the pain, if I am resilient enough," "I can just work slower, and no one will notice."

Many of us are like this. We keep saying yes to our boss, clients, coworkers—but mostly to ourselves—until it is too late. Many of my disability clients had asked themselves these misguided questions too, bringing undue harm to themselves and their families.

THE INFAMOUS "CAN I" QUESTIONS

These questions are wrong because disability is not about whether you can work despite your suffering. It is *not* about whether you can squeeze another workday out of your tired body and soul. Disability is about whether you have an illness that affects your ability to work and make money.

Do not accept the pain and suffering simply because you can "manage." If you must ask "Can I" questions, ask yourself, Can I work without pain and suffering? Can I be productive without further jeopardizing my health? Can I maintain the quality of my work when I go to work sick? If you answer "no" often, you should consider disability income. You must remember you do not live in this world to suffer.

How Much Do You Want to Suffer?

Another question people ask is, "How sick do I have to be to get on disability?" Instead of asking "Can I work while suffering," they now ask, "How much do I have to suffer before I go on disability." Well, how much do you want to suffer?

When I was a young attorney, Mary asked me the same question. She was an interior designer fighting depression. Medications made her hallucinate. She was losing track of projects and time.

"How sick do I have to be to collect disability?" she asked while sitting in my office.

I answered that she could get disability benefits if her symptoms substantially limited her ability to work. She puzzled over the word "substantially."

"Too subjective," Mary said.

It was winter and already dark at 6 p.m. I had to leave. We said goodbye and I went for a swim in the gym next to my office. But I couldn't focus on swimming because my mind kept drifting back to her question. Was there a better way to answer her question? I mentally reviewed my other cases and realized that no one else had asked me that question. They all came ready to apply for disability. This woman, however, wanted to know whether she *should* apply.

Another pattern emerged. My other clients had always come to me during what I call a "disability crisis." A disability crisis is when a worker has lost their job and income due to their disability. They probably have been hospitalized at least once and are in physical and emotional pain. They don't have any income and are scrambling to apply for whatever disability benefits they have left. They've probably missed several deadlines. They are losing their health insurance and facing homelessness. This made sense to me. The nonprofit where I worked prioritized the most urgent cases. It was natural that I received only the most desperate clients. Mary was still working and not in crisis—yet.

We met again a few days later. I told Mary she was different from my other clients because she wasn't in a disability crisis, but she seemed to be getting there.

"Prevention isn't done the last minute," I said. "Look at the signs. Are you having problems at work? Are you completing tasks on time? Have you been written up? How are you with coworkers, customers, your boss? If you go on like this, where do you think you will be?"

Mary admitted she was having many problems at work. If she went on like this, she lamented, she probably would be fired. But for her, disability seemed like such a drastic step. She didn't want to quit her job. She still liked it in some ways. She also didn't want to lose her health insurance from work, but she didn't want to get into a disability crisis either.

I told her she didn't have to quit her job. She had temporary disability benefits, which gave her income, job, and health insurance protections. She could take a *paid medical leave* if she liked.

"Really? I thought all disability was permanent," Mary said. "I didn't know we could go on temporary disability and still keep our job. I didn't know we could get paid beyond our accrued sick and vacation hours. What happens if I don't return to my job after the paid medical leave?"

"You can find a new job or take a longer rest if you need. If you want to take a longer rest, you should apply for Long-Term Disability income. I will help you."

"Am I really sick enough to get on disability?" Mary asked.

"What do you mean by 'sick enough'? How sick do you want to be? How much do you want to suffer? You just told me you're heading toward a disaster. I think that's pretty substantial, don't you? I think you have met the definition of disability."

She sat still, then told me she wanted to take some time to think about it.

A couple of weeks later Mary called me from her therapist's office. The cops almost took her to the emergency room, she said. She was walking into traffic, but she wasn't trying to kill herself. She felt distracted, she explained. She was ready to apply for disability and get on a paid medical leave. She wondered if I would help her. I said yes, naturally.

To Prevent a Disability Crisis, Take a Paid Medical Leave

Mary did not return to her job after her paid medical leave.

She was on Short-Term Disability income for a full year, the maximum benefit period, then transitioned onto Social Security. Because she planned early, she never had a gap in her income. Because she planned early, she maintained her private healthcare coverage until she received Medicare, a type of public health insurance. She was never uninsured. Because she planned early, she knew her Social Security would not cover her expenses, so she moved to a small rural town where her income from Social Security was enough. She was never homeless. Perhaps most importantly, because she planned and acted early, she didn't lose everything to a disability crisis. Planning is the hallmark of a well-executed paid medical leave.

She could have become like my other clients who worked and worked until a full-blown health crisis erupted. She could have been fired, compounding her turmoil. She could have missed applying for Short-Term Disability benefits because she didn't know she had coverage or didn't know she was disabled. She could have missed several months of rent and become homeless. Chaos is the sign of a disability crisis.

What saved Mary? Not waiting until she was sick enough to plan or apply for disability income. Taking a *paid medical leave* as a preventive measure against a *disability crisis*.

Midas, a Karōshi Victim

Why do sick people work until they are demoted or fired? Why don't they take a break? Some even overwork until they die. The Japanese call it 過労死 or karōshi, meaning overwork-death.

Midas wasn't just a rich and powerful king. He was also just like us—an everyday worker. Everything he touched turned into gold.

THE INFAMOUS "CAN I" QUESTIONS

He became the most productive worker in the world! But at the end he died terribly, a karōshi victim.

Our society demands productivity, and we inherit that demand as our own, even as we harm our lives. Midas turned olive trees into gold; we turn rainforests into barren fields. Midas turned food into gold; we poison our fish with mercury, ruin our crops with pesticides. Midas turned his wife and children into gold; we destroy our own relationships.

People judge Midas for his greed. But who doesn't fancy a little alchemy? His vice was ignorance. He didn't know he would turn the living into dead. If he had known better, he would have chosen wiser. We are the same. We want to work hard and succeed—nothing greedy about that. The problem comes when we don't know when to stop. Instead of resting, we overwork. Instead of pursuing protection, we resist it. So many of my disability clients have told me, if they had known better, they would have applied for benefits sooner.

In addition to ignorance, there is guilt. Many clients delay applying for benefits because they feel guilty about not working. They don't want help from others. For them, it is better to suffer than to be guilty.

Guilt, according to psychiatrist David R. Hawkins, is expressed in "shouldn'ts." I shouldn't be sick. I shouldn't be disabled. I shouldn't be an unproductive member of the society. I shouldn't disappoint my coworkers and boss. I shouldn't let my family down.

My good friend, Adam, jokes that the world is ruled by lizard-people and humans are enslaved by them to work, work, work for the pleasure of the humanoid lizards. Their leader is Lord Lizard, who encourages people to overwork and discourages them from cherishing family, friends, health, well-being—everything that resonates with love, which is what Lord Lizard hates the most. Guilt is what Lord Lizard likes us to feel about our human condition; that our body grows old, gets sick, dies. Perhaps it was Lord Lizard who gave Midas the gift of the golden touch. Lord Lizard has other tricks besides guilt. I will warn you on the road ahead.

If you feel guilty about getting sick and taking time off for your health, try self-compassion, a technique taught by Rosanna Franklin, PsyD. It has three steps:

1. Acknowledge the guilty feelings. No matter how they feel, let them be. Don't push them away, don't fuel them—let them dissipate on their own.
2. Acknowledge our common humanity, that all humans go through pain, suffering, self-blame, and guilt. We are not alone in our human condition.
3. Retune the inner voice, shift its tone from harsh and blaming to encouraging and constructive.

You don't have to practice self-compassion alone. Hire a mental health professional to process your guilt. And read David R. Hawkins's book *Letting Go*.

A New Midas

Insurance companies and government agencies like to use adjectives like "substantial" or "marked" to define disability. As my designer client said, such words are subjective. Subjectivity is not a problem per se, but when it is clouded by myths and lies, we end up with horrors such as karōshi. Part of learning is unlearning. That's why you must guard against the lies about disability, like those from Lord Lizard.

When subjectivity is aligned with truth, smart choices follow. If you want to decide wisely on disability, get to know the truth.

THE INFAMOUS "CAN I" QUESTIONS

Once you know the truth, you are a new Midas. Once you become *aware* of truth, you cannot help but make smart choices, regardless of what Lord Lizard dishes out at you.

The truth is:

A great number of us are eligible for disability protections.

Federal and state laws *can* protect our job and health insurance.

Disability insurance *can* replace our lost wages.

They *can*, but if you don't learn to *use* them, they *won't*.

• • •

We don't have to be bedridden, catatonic, or incapacitated to qualify for disability protections.

If we meet the definition of disability, we qualify for benefits.

That definition is not as stringent as many people think.

• • •

Your employer (and the human resources department) is not responsible for counseling you on disability.

They only have to meet certain legal standards.

They are not in the business of helping you get through disability.

You are responsible for knowing, planning, and claiming your own disability protections.

• • •

We are not what we do. Even when we are not working (being "productive"), we are worthy.

There is a time to work, and there is a time to rest and heal.

• • •

When we overwork while sick, our well-being trends down.

If we don't break the downward trend, we get into a crisis.

In a disability crisis, we may lose our job, income, health insurance, home, health, and happiness.

To avert the disability crisis, take a paid medical leave.

• • •

During a paid medical leave, we are under a dome of protections.

Within the dome, our lost wages are replaced by disability income. Our job and health insurance are secured by state and federal laws.

Within the dome, we can safely plan our future and ask meaningful questions like:

Do we want to stop working for a while?

Should we go back to work after a short break?

Is my job killing me?

Do I need to reconnect with my loved ones, or my life?

• • •

There is no magic formula, algorithm, or bright line rule as to when you should stop working. As you learn more, you choose wiser. That is how this book can help you.

Toward the end, it is you who decide. Don't let others choose for you; no one can tell you what to do. Your doctors and lawyers may advise you, but it is you with an unclouded heart who should decide. It is *your* art of rest, after all. May you become a new Midas: guilt free, more aware.

CHAPTER 2

A Model Definition of Mental Disability

This chapter is on mental illness and disability. What exactly is mental illness, and when does it become disabling? Before we begin, remember we discuss these issues in the context of disability income. You may have come across other ideas and definitions on mental illness and disability, but they may not apply in our context. We are specifically interested in these issues in the disability claim process.

• • •

Let's begin with a definition.

Disability is when you have an illness that affects your work and income.

This is a simple sentence, but it turns out to be a model definition of disability. All disability income benefits use some variation of this definition, whether they are Public or Commercial Insurance, individual or group policies, Short- or Long-Term Disability benefits, federal or state programs. To understand this definition is to understand the essence of disability income. It has three parts: **illness, work, income**. Let's discuss each of them.

Illness

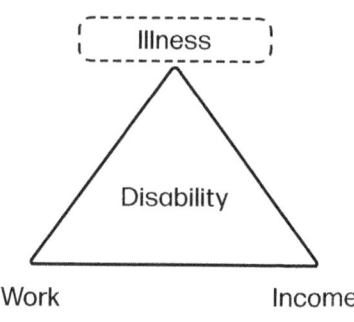

Life has ups and downs, naturally. Sometimes we feel sad or guilty, other times joy and peace. Sometimes our thinking is chaotic and negative, other times bright and harmonious. So, what makes negative feelings and thoughts illnesses, as opposed to just a natural part of everyday life? In the world of disability, we look for three things: 1) persistent symptoms, 2) interference with work and daily life, and 3) medical documentation. When all three are present, an illness exists.

1. Persistent Symptoms

Imagine you live in a castle and your thoughts and feelings are like rooms you can visit. One day you visit a room of sadness. That's all right. We all have good days and bad days. You know you are not your sadness, just like you know you are not the room you visit. You are confident that you will leave the room, and eventually you do, on your own or with the help of others.

But sometimes you have problems leaving a room. You may overidentify with the room, not believing you can leave. You may blame yourself for being sick or deny your symptoms altogether. You may decline the help you need to leave, like medical care and disability protections. Your sadness becomes persistent; you are stuck in a room. *Persistency* of symptoms is a sign of mental illness.

Below are some negative feelings and thoughts. They are grouped in constellations that make up *types* of mental illnesses. Get to know them. Name them. If you feel stuck in a constellation (or two), your symptoms may have become persistent.

- *Depression.* Irritable. Disinterested in life. Hopeless. Guilty. Shameful. Suicidal. Tired. Sad. Withdrawn. Lack of appetite. Huge weight gain or loss. Moody. Can't focus.
- *Neurocognitive Disorders.* Forgetful. Scattered. Disorganized. Confused. Indecisive. Insensitive.
- *Schizophrenia.* Delusional. Hearing voices. Seeing shadows. Emotionless. Isolated. Moody. Odd beliefs and behaviors. Loss of interest and pleasure.
- *Anxiety.* Obsessive. Compulsive. Excessive worries. Fear. Denial. Restless. Scattered. Hyper-vigilant. Anxious. Insomnia. Panic attacks.
- *Psychosomatic Disorders.* Mysterious pain. Fear of getting sick. Strange sensations. Tired. Anxious. Odd bodily movements.
- *Personality Disorders.* Suspicious. Odd beliefs. Detached. Withdrawn. Hypersensitive. Attention seeking. Perfectionist. Rage. Frequent social conflicts.
- *Autistic.* Socially awkward. Can't reciprocate. Can't communicate. Uneven development of skills. Unusual responses to light and sound. Hyperactive. Inattentive. Impulsive. Aggressive. Self-injurious.
- *Eating Disorders.* Starving oneself. Preoccupied with body shape and weight. Binge eating. Self-induced vomiting.

Excessive exercise. Laxatives. Moody. Withdrawn. Irritable. Amenorrhea.

- *Trauma.* Stressful memories. Flashbacks. Nightmares. Avoidant Behavior. Moody. Fear. Angry. Anxious. Aggressive. Cold.

- *Addiction.* Intense urges. Overspending money on addiction. Reckless behavior. Committing crimes for addictive substances. Withdrawal symptoms. Cannot stop using despite consequences.

2. Interference with Work and Daily Life

Here is a hypothetical for you. Your best friend at work, Peter, confides in you that he feels sad and anxious "all the time." You are surprised, because he appears to be on top of the world. He just got promoted and has a loving wife and two beautiful young kids. Everyone seems to adore him. He asks you if you or others notice he is "losing it." You tell him that he looks fine and reassure him that his difficult feelings will pass.

A few weeks later, the office throws Peter a party for being best employee of the year. You meet his wife at the party, and she tells you how much she loves Peter and what a great father he is. The day after that, Peter comes to you and complains again about his sadness and anxiety. You are puzzled because he is such a lucky guy in every way. He asks: *Do I have a mental illness?* What would you say?

Yes, you may say, he has mental illness. Using the castle metaphor above, Peter is clearly stuck in a room, even if you don't know at which constellation(s). He seems to have depression, but also some anxiety disorder. Perhaps he has both.

Or you may say no, because although he seems stuck, he is living well personally and professionally. Many psychologists would agree with you. To them, if Peter's symptoms do not interfere with his work and daily life, then he is not mentally ill, at least not seriously.

For the purpose of disability income, the definition of mental illness *always* includes interference with work and daily activities, also known as "functional limitations." Later, we will discuss what these limitations are and how to document and report them.

3. Medical Documentation

The mental illness must be documented by a healthcare provider or it doesn't count—at least not in the disability income world. It sounds strange, but you are not officially sick until you see a doctor.

As someone who has been through the mental healthcare system, my friend Adam occasionally jokes that before his psychotherapist diagnosed him with depression, he was just moody. After the diagnosis, he had a "medical condition." Of course, his illness didn't worsen at the moment of diagnosis, but it was verified and validated.

If you want to apply for disability but are not seeing a healthcare provider, do so immediately. A healthcare provider can be your primary care doctor or mental health specialist such as a psychologist or psychiatrist. If you apply for disability without a healthcare provider on your side, the insurer will use its own medical professionals to examine you, an obviously biased situation. Or worse, the insurer will deny your application because you haven't provided adequate evidence that you are suffering from a mental illness and obtaining appropriate care.

Summary

In the world of disability income, a mental illness must:

1. Have persistent symptoms,
2. Interfere with work and daily life, and
3. Be medically documented.

A few notes on mental disability

Your mental illness can be sudden or chronic. A long history of documented illnesses is helpful but not required for disability claims. Severity is the key: Are your symptoms severe enough to cause functional limitations? Do they limit your ability to work? Do they require medical attention?

Illness includes side effects from your medications. Psych meds can cause people to feel tired, anxious, depressed, and, in some cases, to hallucinate. Don't forget to mention these side effects to your provider; they can help you qualify for disability.

The disabling illness doesn't have to be work related. This is not worker's compensation. However, if you apply for both disability income and worker's compensation and end up getting both, you will most likely have to return some disability income. This is called "offset" or "subrogation" and exists in most Commercial Insurance policies.

A Commercial Insurance policy can exclude certain illnesses from coverage. For example, it may exclude mental illnesses you have had prior to the coverage. These illnesses are called pre-existing conditions. However, most exclusion do not last forever. Once the exclusion expires, you can apply based on that illness.

Disability claims involving drug and alcohol addictions are subject to heightened scrutiny, although addiction is a medical condition. Many insurers will deny a claim if they believe that the claimant is willfully harming himself with drugs or alcohol and causing his own disability. Social Security is one of these insurers. Before 1996, addiction qualified for Social Security disability benefits. But after the 1996 Personal Responsibility Act, Social Security began denying addiction-related claims. If you have a history of drug or alcohol addiction, consult an attorney to see how it may affect your disability claim.

Not only do insurers undermine mental illness, but people with mental illness often deny it as well. They dismiss it as unreal or something trivial that can be overcome by free will. They even feel guilty for having it. They don't want to have mental illness, let alone be disabled by it. But poor mental health is one of the leading causes of disability. It is the second most common reason for Social Security disability, right behind skeletomuscular diseases. As common as it is, many people still cannot accept mental disability. My client Jim was one of them.

• • •

Jim's Story

It had been raining for days when Jim showed up at my office with a wet letter. I peeled the pages off one by one until I found a notice of approval from Social Security. "Jim, good news! Your disability claim is approved!"

"No! It is not good news. It says I am disabled because of my anxiety. I am not disabled because of my anxiety. I am disabled because of my back pain!"

"Your back pain is not enough to qualify you for Social Security disability," I explained, "but you have plenty of medical evidence for a mental health claim." I reminded him of his psychiatric hospitalization, which turned the case around.

"I could work if I wanted to, if not for the back pain!"

He was adamant that his anxiety was under control. He was not crazy.

"Andy, you better get this fixed!"

I told him that it was foolish to appeal just to switch the medical condition. He would get more retroactive pay on the mental health claim. He would get Medicare sooner. I advised him to talk with his therapist instead. He stood up, said he planned to report me to the state bar, and slammed the door behind him. Moments later, I heard someone shouting from the street below. I looked out the window and saw him running across the road, yelling at the cars, splashing water everywhere.

A few days later, I got a call from Jim's social worker, Molly. "Jim wants me to tell you he is not going to report you to the state bar," Molly said in her Brooklyn accent. "He is afraid of being judged as a malingerer. [A malingerer is someone who fakes symptoms to gain some unfair advantage, such as feel good drugs or income benefits.] Jim says he is sorry and will come see you soon. Wait, actually, he wants to speak to you now, can he come now?"

"Is it a good idea?" I muttered. "It will rain soon."

"He says it is a *great* idea and he will be there in fifteen minutes," Molly continued. "He is just walking there from my office."

He arrived in exactly fifteen minutes to explain that where he grew up in the Midwest, mental illness didn't "satisfy" as a reason for disability. It wasn't as "real" as physical illness. If someone had it, they better "suck it up" and get back to work. It was something to be overcome by sheer will.

He talked about his alcoholic father who started binge drinking after Jim's mother died of brain cancer. His father applied for disability based on depression, but the insurance company denied the claim, judging his father a malingerer. His family broke apart soon after. Ever since, Jim would cringe when he heard the words malingerer or malingering. He was glad they were uncommon words.

"Uncommon and damning," I said.

"But I *knew* dad's mental illness was real," Jim said. "I can't believe I have it too. I am so ashamed."

He burst into tears and buried his face in his hands. "I am so sorry, Andy. I've made so many mistakes!"

It really did start to rain.

• • •

Loss of Income

To qualify for disability income, you must have a loss of income from work. But you may not have to lose *all* your income to qualify—some disability income allows partial disability.

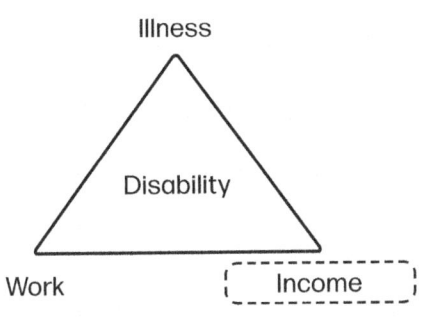

If you reduced your work hours due to your illness, resulting in a loss of income, you should apply for disability.

Similarly, if you switch to a lower-paying job due to your illness, that is also considered a loss of income. But if the new job pays the same, you don't have a loss of income. Remember, disability income replaces lost wages. No loss, no replacement.

You don't necessarily have to use up all your accrued sick hours to have a loss of income. Many disability insurances will pay benefits even if you have enough sick hours to cover your entire leave. You can save these hours for later use. You can also spend some of your sick hours while you wait for your disability income to kick in. This helps you avoid a gap in income. You can even integrate your sick time with your disability benefits to get full pay (more on this later).

Speaking of income, you don't have to be poor to apply for disability. Some people think all disability income is welfare (i.e., "free money"); that is not true. There are only two major welfare disability programs: Supplemental Security Income (SSI) and California's Cash Assistance Program for Immigrants (CAPI). Most disability benefits operate as *insurance*, not welfare. If you get into a car accident, would you be reluctant to claim insurance because you are rich?

Effect on Work

To qualify for disability income, your illness must affect your work. The effect cannot be slight. It must be significant enough to decrease your income. But it doesn't have to be so significant that you can't do anything. I said this

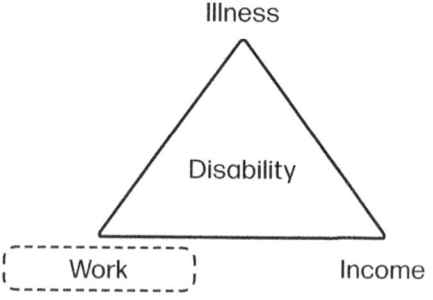

before, but I will say it again. You don't have to be bedridden to get on disability. You don't have to be under the protection and observation of a psych ward. Don't fall into the trap of asking wrong questions. Don't work until you succumb to a health crisis. If you have an illness that affects your work, and it affects you so much that you have lost income or will likely lose income, plan on applying for disability. Still not sure? Consider this example.

George is an attorney with a brain injury. He physically can get to work but is limited in performing his duties. He is slow to finish his legal research and misses deadlines. He cannot contain his emotions and lashes out at others, even clients. His employer is willing to give him some slack but will not put him in front of a jury. He is about to exhaust his Paid Time Off (PTO) and may request unpaid leave soon.

What do you think? Can George work? You may say yes, he can work, because he still can function as an attorney, albeit at a lower efficiency. With some adjustments, he still can work. For example, his employer can give him more time to do research and limit his contact with clients and opposing counsel (maybe). On the other hand, you may say no, because you think that George cannot work as an attorney if he can't function socially, meet deadlines, and operate in a courtroom.

Don't bother debating this issue because the question is irrelevant. When it comes to the effect on work, the applicable question is not whether someone can work (we have talked about these "Can I" questions before). Rather, the real question is whether someone's illness affects his ability to work and earn income.

Whether George can work if he is allowed extra time to finish is not the right question. Whether George can work if the employer is willing to give him less client-facing work is not the right question. The right question is: Does his illness affect his ability to work and earn income? In George's case, the answer is clearly yes. Therefore, George should apply for disability income.

The wrong question makes you think in black and white: you either can work or you can't work. It also makes you jump to a conclusion. If you can work, why would you consider disability income? The right question opens up possibilities. The right question is the model definition itself: "Do I have an illness that affects my work and income?" If yes, then you may have a disability claim.

• • •

Now that you have learned the model definition, what do you think of the folks below? Are they good candidates for disability income? Use the Triangle of Definition (of disability) below to help you answer.

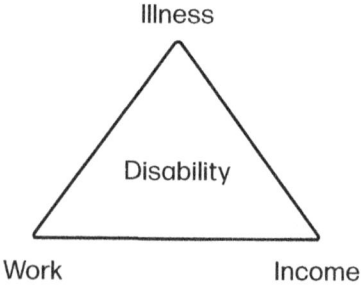

1. Gil, a factory worker, recently developed post-traumatic stress disorder (PTSD). Flashbacks interrupt his concentration and make operating machinery dangerous. His doctor suggests one month of medical leave. He has accrued enough sick hours to last a couple of months.

2. Gidon, a manager, is diagnosed with depression after the death of his wife. While he can physically get to work, he has difficulty making decisions and relating to his subordinates. He is short on accrued sick and vacation time and may need to take an unpaid leave.
3. Midori, a saleswoman, quits her job because she has anxiety disorder and can no longer socially interact with customers. Her employer offers her a job as a stock clerk that requires no customer interactions. She takes that job as well as a large pay cut.
4. Itzhak, a coder, has problems completing his work due to the side effects of his medication. He has schizophrenia. Without the medication, he would hallucinate and harm himself. He is not sure whether he qualifies for disability because it is the side effects of his medication, not the symptoms of schizophrenia, that prevent him from working.
5. Hilary, a construction worker, recently developed obsessive compulsive disorder (OCD). Construction noises debilitate her. Her employer offers her a sedentary job in the accounting office that pays the same. She accepts the offer.
6. Kyung Wha, a dance teacher, is due to give birth in five months. She wonders if she can get disability benefits due to pregnancy. She has a family history of postpartum depression.
7. David, a physical trainer, hasn't worked in a couple of years due to a severe eating disorder. He doesn't think he qualifies for disability benefits because he gets plenty of money from passive investment.

Answers:

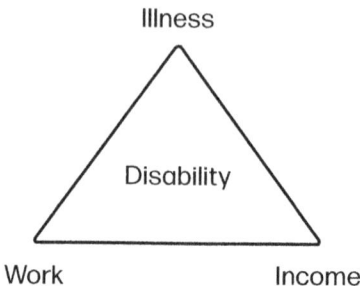

1. Gil is a good candidate because he meets the three angles: illness, effect on work, and the loss of income. Depending on his insurance plans, he may not have to deplete all his accrued sick hours before qualifying for disability.
2. Gidon is a good candidate because his illness affects his work and income. The fact that he can physically get to work doesn't matter; we are looking for limitations on work duties and we see them.
3. Midori is a good candidate because she has lost income due to a medical condition that affects her work. Just because she gets another job doesn't mean she cannot be disabled and get disability income.
4. Itzhak is a good candidate because his illness affects his ability to work and make money. Side effects from his medication are part of his illness.
5. Hilary is not a good candidate because she has no loss of income. Disability income is an income replacement tool. No loss of income, no disability benefits.
6. Kyung Wha is a good candidate for disability. Most short-term disability insurances recognize pregnancy as a medical condition and pay benefits for a few weeks

before and after childbirth. She may extend her disability benefits beyond the few weeks if she develops long-lasting postpartum depression.
7. David is a good candidate because his medical condition affects his ability to work and make money. The fact that he has income from investment is irrelevant *unless* he is applying for welfare programs.

CHAPTER 3

Telling Your Story

I said I would show you how to document evidence but that's just legalese for telling your story. The better your story, the more likely you will be approved. The Adjudicator is the person (or team) at the insurer who decides whether you are disabled. They expect your story to be told in a certain way and by certain professionals. In this chapter you will learn how.

Your story is both biographic and autobiographic. Your primary biographers are your healthcare providers: primary care doctor, nurses, specialists, psychologists, therapists, psychiatrists, etc. To save time I call them "doctors." You may also have secondary biographers, such as social workers, case managers, friends, and family. What they say and write about you can also become evidence. But you should focus on the doctors; help them tell an accurate and supportive story about you.

In some disability claims, especially the longer ones, you will need to complete questionnaires about yourself. That's what I call autobiographical. The form wants to know about your functional limitations (i.e., activities of daily living).

Remember, stories (not legalese) move people. Disability Adjudicators are people too.

• • •

Let's talk about getting you a biographer (or two). To receive disability benefits, your illness must be diagnosed and documented by a doctor, preferably, *your* doctor. If you don't have a regular doctor, get one immediately. Otherwise, the Adjudicator will send you to their own doctor. I often give this analogy: it is like you had a car accident and the insurance company of the other driver is sending you to their own doctor to examine your injuries (professionally called consultative examinations). Do you think they will be fair? Get your own doctor.

Get a psychotherapist who provides talk therapy. They usually spend about fifty minutes with you at each session, a length of time you don't get with a primary care doctor. That extra time gives you time to tell your story.

See a mental health specialist to certify your disability paperwork. If you claim disability based on mental health, ask a psychiatrist or psychologist to sign your paperwork, not a proctologist. Having a specialist conveys to the insurer that your mental illness is serious and requires an expert. If the Adjudicator challenges your mental health claim, you have a specialist on your side. Generalists like your primary care doctor can sign your disability paperwork, but their support may not be enough. If you are applying for Long-Term Disability based on mental health, definitely see a mental health specialist.

Degrees also matter. Insurers readily accept the following degrees for disability paperwork: medical doctor (MD), doctor of osteopathic medicine (DO), doctor of philosophy (PhD), and doctor of psychology (PsyD). Other degrees, such as registered nurse (RN), master's degrees (e.g., MSW) or licensed clinical social worker (LCSW) may or may not be enough. But you still can *and should* work with the latter group. Just make sure you have someone with the acceptable credentials to sign off on your paperwork. The two types of professionals can and often do work as a team. For example, the provider with an MD prescribes the psychiatric medications while your therapist with an MSW provides psychoanalysis, and together they can sign your disability paperwork (co-sign).

You want a sympathetic biographer, so choose a medical provider who hears and understands you. If you don't feel that way about your doctor, talk to her about it. If things don't change, find a good time to switch to another doctor. A good time is when you don't need a doctor to sign off on your paperwork immediately. A brand-new doctor may not be comfortable completing disability paperwork for a brand-new patient.

• • •

Would the following statements apply to you?

"When I am in front of my doctor, I don't remember what to say."

Or

"My doctor asks me how I am, I say I am fine. The visit is pretty short. It's like this every time."

Or

"I have seen my doctor for years. He should know everything about me. I don't feel like I have to repeat everything every time."

If yes, then you might have the same problem as Susan.

Susan's Story

Susan was in her late thirties and sold expensive furniture for a living. She considered herself "positive" and was "surprised" that Dr. Angel, her primary care doctor, thought she had depression. She was adamant she would return to work after a short break, and the depression would vanish as quickly as it had come.

Dr. Angel referred her to see Dr. Nehru, a psychiatrist, and she did. For a while, things seemed stable until one summer morning, she thought about suicide. She postponed returning to work. She got on disability, received a few months of payments before the insurance company said she had recovered and should go back to work. They stopped her disability checks. That's when she came to me for help.

"When I am in front of my psychiatrist, I don't remember what to say." Susan explained in my office.

"Your psychiatrist, Dr. Nehru, mostly wrote you were 'doing fine. no new symptoms.' He even wrote you had 'bright affect' on several visits."

"Oh, did he?"

"So why are you disabled, Susan? You look fine and that's what you have been telling your doctors," I closed her psychiatric records and pushed them back to her.

"You know, Andy, when you sell $50,000 chairs, you can't afford to have a sad face."

"I doubt Dr. Nehru will buy a chair from you."

"That's only because you don't know how good I am."

She laughed at her own joke, then said, "You must know I came from a pretty tough childhood." I nodded, I knew from her psych records that her parents were poor, and she struggled to finish school. But she had a knack for sales and had done well for herself in New York and Paris. Even as she sat in my office talking about her own depression, she still looked upbeat in a sapphire blue dress.

"Positive thinking brings positive results. The secret law of attraction! I didn't get to where I am by moping around."

"Susan, you have to tell Dr. Nehru your symptoms. The same ones that you are telling me. Difficulty concentrating. Sleeplessness. Fatigue. Feelings of guilt and hopelessness."

"I will try. Our visits are very short, twenty minutes max. I don't really have the time to get into things."

"You must be mindful about it. When you see your doctor, it is a golden opportunity to share your story. Don't go in without a purpose. Set up an intent to report your symptoms and be prepared. Make a list if you must. Keep a diary. And please report your functional limitations as well."

"What's the difference between symptoms and functional limitations?"

"Think of the limitations as examples of what you can't do. You said sometimes you are so exhausted you don't wake up and groom. That's a functional limitation."

"I don't know if I want to discuss that."

"Why?"

"It's embarrassing."

"It's the truth. It's evidence. Don't put on a good face for Dr. Nehru. It's not going to help your case."

"You think I put on a good face for him? And why would I do that?"

"Because you just told me it's embarrassing."

"Oh, oh. I guess I am putting on a good face. Hmm. That's so interesting."

"When I ask my clients why they are disabled, it's not uncommon for them to give me many reasons. But when I review their medical records, I don't see those reasons. Perhaps it is because doctors are authority figures, and patients find them too intimidating for honesty. Maybe the patient likes the doctor and doesn't want to disappoint her. A colleague suggested 'resilience.' People are so resilient that they forget how much they have adapted to their pain and suffering. They've 'moved on.' Others just don't want to complain anymore. Or they are afraid they won't be believed, especially for women, who are often questioned and disbelieved and called 'complainers.' In any event, for various reasons, many people end up minimizing their symptoms in front of their medical providers, telling them that they are 'fine,' and that's what ends up in the progress notes, the same progress notes that the Adjudicator at the insurance company will review. If the records keep stating that you are fine, why should the Adjudicator approve your claim?"

"I see. What about the time I shut myself in the house for three days because I felt too wretched inside after talking to my hateful ex-boyfriend? I couldn't cook, couldn't shop, couldn't talk to friends and family? Those are functional limitations?"

"Yes, they are. And I like how descriptive it is. You didn't just claim, I can't cook. You described an event. Jot down more of these events and report them to your doctors."

"Or how about this: instead of just saying I couldn't focus I could add that sometimes I feel so scattered people have to repeat the same thing to me several times!"

"Yes!"

"Or instead of saying I couldn't do my job I could explain how my job required a lot of traveling and public speaking and my fatigue makes these tasks impossible."

"Yes! But stay away from all-or-nothing terms like always, never, impossible."

She slouched into the chair and exhaled. "Gosh, getting on disability requires a lot of work. Such a catch-22. You have to be able to prove you are disabled."

"Yes, it can feel like doing two opposite things at the same time. On one hand, you need to get a lot of tasks done to qualify: Find out what benefits you are eligible for. File claims on time. Fill out the forms correctly. Report symptoms and limitations. Get the doctor to complete the paperwork. Get the medical records to the insurance company. And if you are denied, repeat the process on appeal. On the other hand, you are trying to prove you can't focus, can't get things done, can't get along with people. But Susan, remember, being disabled from work is not being disabled from life. You can be strong *and* disabled. You can be resilient *and* vulnerable. To win your claim, you must tell others about your suffering."

She seemed lost in thought, then said, "Yes. I can get through this. I need my strength and resilience more than ever. I need to be vulnerable and communicative more than ever. I can be strong and disabled. I can be resilient and vulnerable." She closed her eyes and repeated the last sentence three times like a mantra.

"Yes! And have you thought about getting a therapist?"

"Hmm, think I should?"

"Yes. A therapist can help you dive deeper into your issues."

"I have more issues than *Time* magazine!" She laughed at her own joke again, and I tried to laugh with her.

"Now I feel bad about all those missed appointments with my doctors. I should've taken better care of myself." She sighed and closed her eyes. Tears fell.

"It's okay, Susan. That's one interesting thing about disability claims, the evidence can come from the future or the past. You can start building up your case today." I handed her a tissue.

"Yes, be present. Thank you, Andy."

• • •

To Your Doctor: Symptoms and Limitations

Susan's story illustrates why some claimants with serious illness look fine on paper (so their claims are denied). Their limitations never got into the medical records. Nobody understood why they were disabled, including their doctors. To win your disability case, help others understand why. To understand your disability means to empathize with your symptoms and functional limitations.

Symptoms are your subjective experience of your illness. It is natural to have negative thoughts and feelings from time to time, but if you feel that way constantly, then you may be psychologically stuck and have a mental illness.

Functional limitations are limitations in activities of daily living, such as inability to groom, shop, focus, read, write, and socialize.

Here we come to another triangle: the Triangle of Understanding.

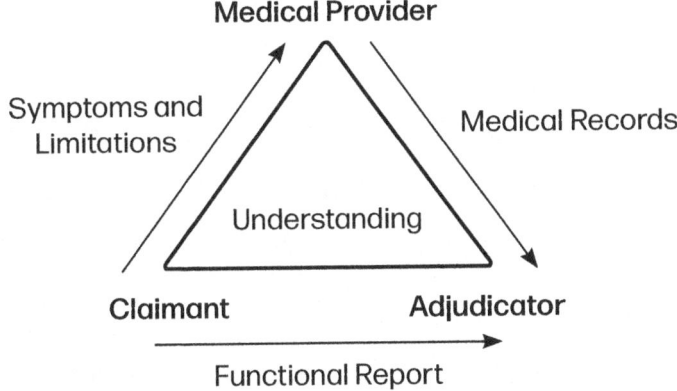

The triangle depicts how information about your disability goes from the source (you) to the Adjudicator. This flow of information helps others understand your disability. When you report your symptoms and functional limitations to your doctor, the information becomes part of the medical record. The medical record also includes things you don't personally say to your doctor, like your lab results, MRI reports, discharge summary, etc. The medical record then goes to the Adjudicator as medical evidence.

If you don't report your symptoms and functional limitations to your doctor, she can't understand why you are disabled. If your doctor doesn't understand your disability, she can't document it properly, she won't complete your disability form properly, and she may even doubt your disability.

If your doctor doesn't understand why you are disabled, your Adjudicator probably won't either and your disability claim will fail. Therefore, you must vigilantly report your symptoms and functional limitations. Here are some tips on how to report them effectively.

Report symptoms and limitations at every visit

Every time you see your doctor, report all your symptoms and limitations. Every time. Not once in a while. Not every other time. *Every time.* To win a disability claim, you need a trail of clinical notes pointing toward your disability.

Don't let familiarity fool you. If you have a long relationship with your doctor, you may get too cozy and stop reporting your symptoms and limitations. After all, you have known each other for years, right? She should know what is going on, right? So instead of consistently reporting your illness, you talk about each other's life, the kids, politics—like you are talking to your old friend. Only she is not your friend. And now your record is empty of your latest symptoms and limitations, events that showcase your disability.

Keep in mind that she is your medical provider. On the one hand, she provides health care to you. On the other hand, she provides medical evidence for your disability claim. She is the storyteller of your story to the insurer. Let her tell the Adjudicator about your disability, not your politics or dinner parties.

Don't underreport your illness

Sometimes people puzzle over this advice. They think, why would anyone underreport their symptoms to their doctors? But it happens all the time, as it did with Susan. She put on a good face for her doctor, just as she put on a good face for her clients. She undermined her own symptoms, which damaged her disability claim. Why do people do this? Perhaps due to resilience, like I mentioned to Susan.

TELLING YOUR STORY

Or they don't want to complain.

Or they are afraid the doctor won't believe them.

Or they are shy.

Or they are embarrassed about their illness. (Lord Lizard operates here.)

Or they subscribed to "positive thinking," like Susan.

So they minimize their illness to their doctor, saying they are "fine." And that's what ends up in the progress notes, "the patient is fine." The same progress notes that the Adjudicator will review when they apply for disability. Like I said to Susan, if the records keep stating that you are fine, why should the Adjudicator approve your claim?

Be honest and explicit with your doctors about your pain and suffering. Discuss any inability to concentrate, remember simple instructions, spend time with others, and regulate emotions. If you have physical illnesses as well, discuss any inability to sit, stand, walk, crawl, crouch, using your fingers, lift, pull, etc. Report examples of what you cannot do, such as the inability to complete daily chores like cooking, laundry, going to religious gatherings, etc.

By reporting symptoms, limitations, and examples accurately, you will develop a trail of evidence for a disability claim. And even if you never end up applying for disability, don't you want your doctors to know what's really going on with you so that they can help you get better?

If what you really mean to say is your illness remains the same, then say exactly that.

If what you really mean to say is you have been having good days and bad days, then say exactly that.

But don't say, "I'm fine."

On the other hand, exaggeration can damage your claim. If your illness appears excessive, the Adjudicator may consider you a malingerer. As mentioned in Jim's story, malingering is when someone lies about his illness to get something, such as addictive drugs and disability income.

Adjudicators are always scanning for signs of malingering. They compare different sets of records for inconsistencies. They judge whether your complaints are medically reasonable. They dish out psychological tests for malingering. They may even send an investigator to spy on you.

Be descriptive with your functional limitations

Help your doctor document your disability by reporting specific examples of your limitations. If you don't give them the specifics, all your doctor has is a vague sense that you cannot work because you are sick. Here are some examples of generic report vs. specific report.

> Generic: I cannot do my job because I feel anxious.
>
> vs.
>
> Specific: My job requires a lot of business travel and public speaking, and my agoraphobia makes it impossible for me to perform these duties.
>
> Generic: I cannot work because I feel tired all the time.
>
> vs.

Specific: My job requires me to lift at least twenty-five pounds throughout the day and be on my feet constantly. I am no longer able to perform these activities because of low energy.

Here is a list of mental functions required at work. Mark the ones that are required at your job. Mark the ones that are affected by your mental illness. If you have two marks next to a function, then you have found a limitation.

Mental functions
- Remember facts, people, and places
- Understand simple or detailed instructions
- Perform simple or detailed instructions
- Maintain focus for an extended period
- Maintain attendance
- Maintain schedule
- Be punctual
- Sustain routine without special supervision
- Work with others without being distracted by them
- Interact appropriately with the public
- Handle criticism
- Get along with coworkers
- Maintain neatness and cleanliness
- Respond appropriately to changes
- Respond to hazards and avoid them
- Travel to unfamiliar places and use public transportation
- Set goals and plans

If you have physical limitations, check the list below. Mental illness can affect physical functions too. For example, depression and psychotropic medications can cause low energy and limit physical activities.

Physical functions
- Climbing and balancing
- Fingering and feeling objects
- Kneeling and crawling
- Reaching and handling
- Stooping and crouching
- Pushing and pulling
- Hearing
- Speaking
- Seeing
- Lifting and carrying
- Standing
- Walking
- Sitting

These lists, adapted from Social Security disability regulations, are not exhaustive. They are to help you think about typical functions at work.

After specifying the functions, quantify. How long can you stand? How long can you sit? How often are you late? How short is your attention span? How many days of work do you miss per week? How many days are you late per week?

Describe memorable events

Which of these statements would leave a stronger impression on the Adjudicator?

The patient has outbursts in public.

Yesterday, the patient screamed on a bus, threw garbage on the driver, and was arrested.

The second one is more likely to stay in the mind of the Adjudicator (and affect him). Give your biographer-doctor something memorable to write about. But don't go overboard. Your record shouldn't read like a medical thriller either.

Clarify the record

Mental health can be a fuzzy matter, and the insurer may use that fuzziness against the insured (you). For example, if a disability policy excludes work-related mental health illnesses (e.g., work stress), and the medical record is unclear whether the symptoms are work related, then the insurer may argue that they are indeed work related and deny the claim.

To address this issue, work with your doctor to clarify the record. For example, identify what worsens your illness. Are they all work related? Or is there an underlying illness that's beyond work stress? Give your doctor enough information so that she can reasonably opine whether your disability is work related. (If your mental illness is mostly caused by work, you may need to apply for worker's compensation instead.)

Verify your own medical records and confirm receipt

One time, I met with a new client who had an upcoming disability hearing at Social Security. Social Security denied his case because of his methamphetamine use. By the time the client came to me, he had stopped using methamphetamine for almost a year. However, he still had severe depression. I told him the meth-free period would be good for his hearing, because it demonstrated that his depression existed independent of his drug use.

A week later, I was disappointed when I received his medical records. They showed the client was actively using meth. Puzzled, I contacted the client to clarify the story. The client assured me he had stopped and called the doctor. The doctor called me, apologizing that the progress notes were wrong. He had been copying and pasting the notes to save time and the misinformation on meth was carried over from the previous visits.

Mistakes happen. Verify your medical records. Under the federal law the Health Insurance Portability and Accountability Act of 1996 (HIPAA), you have the right to receive copies of your medical record and correct any errors. In this case, the client had the doctor amend the progress notes, and we submitted a letter to Social Security to explain the issue.

Finally, make sure the Adjudicator receives copies of your medical record. Seems simple enough, but many cases are denied simply because the Adjudicator didn't receive the medical records. These are the unfortunate "lack of medical evidence" denials. Don't let it happen to you.

To Your Insurer: The Function Report

Now let's talk about your autobiography: what you write about yourself. On Short-Term Disability claims, you may not have to write much; sometimes you just answer one or two questions while filing the initial claim. But on longer disability claims, the Adjudicator will ask more questions and may send you a stand-alone questionnaire called the Function Report.

The Function Report asks about your activities of daily living, such as cleaning, cooking, shopping, paying bills, grooming yourself, reading, focusing, enjoying hobbies, socializing, and caring for pets or children or other dependents. If you see these types of questions, know that this is basically a Function Report, even if the insurer calls it by another name, such as Daily Activities Questionnaire.

Many people find the Function Report confusing. Some questions sound irrelevant, others black and white (think "Can I" questions transposed to "Can you" interrogatories), while others sound rather generic (and bland). But that's okay. I will show you how to handle these mindboggling questions below. A properly completed Function Report can help the Adjudicator understand your disability. It forms the base of the Triangle of Understanding.

You may need to complete the Function Report when you first apply and later on to maintain your disability status. The longer your claim, the more times you have to complete it. However, even if you just want Short-Term Disability, read the following. It will help you understand what evidence the Adjudicator wants, as the nature of the evidence is same for both Short- and Long-Term Disability.

Work With Your Attorney

First, if you are represented by an attorney, complete the Function Report with your attorney. Do NOT send the form to the Adjudicator without your attorney's approval. Let your attorney submit the form to the Adjudicator. If you need more time to complete the form, let the attorney ask for the extension. If the Adjudicator calls you, tell her to call the attorney instead. All communications with the Adjudicator go through your attorney.

The attorney does all the talking, and that includes talking through you and you through him. You talk through him as he presents your case to the world. He talks through you because your answers are informed and transformed by his legal knowledge and experience. The attorney is like a ghostwriter who has helped many people write successful autobiographies. You have the content, but he knows how to present it to the audience. It is your life, your truth, but it is his show.

Beware of "No Problem"

Sometimes claimants wonder why the insurer would ask questions about their shopping, cooking, or volunteering at church. They think I cannot work, but I can take care of myself at home, so they casually write "no problem" or just not answer them.

The insurer asks these seemingly irrelevant questions to gauge what you (the insured) can and cannot perform at work. For example, a question about whether you volunteer at church translates to whether you can work as a team. A question about whether you can carry groceries translates to whether you can lift light objects.

If you write "no problem," the insurer will conclude you have no limitations performing similar tasks at a work setting. If you don't answer, you miss a chance at explaining your disability.

Make Copies

If you get a paper copy of the Function Report, make a copy of it so that you can practice on it. Yes, treat it initially as a scrapbook. Poke a hole in it for your frustration. Triple circle the confusing questions, star the relevant ones. Comment on the side margin or leave a question for your lawyer. Doodle. Draw your face of pain.

But that's not the copy you submit. The copy you submit looks so clean it shines. The answers on it are relevant, concise, and true.

Be Truthful and Descriptive

The Adjudicator will compare your answers with your medical records. If you give extreme answers like "I never go outside due to my disability," the Adjudicator will search your medical records to refute or verify. If the Adjudicator finds frequent discrepancies, she may doubt your credibility, and delay or deny your claim.

Instead of extreme (all-or-nothing) answers, you can qualify your answers with a time frame. For example, you can say "every three to four days, I feel so tired I stay in bed the whole day." If you cannot work every three to four days, then you cannot hold a common, competitive full-time job.

Commercial insurers routinely spy on their claimants and videorecord their activities. The goal is to catch the claimant doing something he says he cannot do on the Function Report. Also be careful of what you put on social media such as Facebook or Instagram. Insurers monitor those too.

Honor Your Adaptation

Sometimes people don't report symptoms and limitations that they have adapted to. Take low energy, a depressive symptom, for example. Folks with low energy may take frequent breaks throughout the day to adapt. Frequent resting becomes habitual, then ordinary, then part of life. Forgotten and not reported.

Spiritually, it makes sense. Regardless of obstacles, we feel resilient, and we don't want to dwell on the negative. But to win a claim, you must describe all your symptoms and limitations, including those you cope with. Honor how you have made every day livable (even lovable) by revealing your adaptations. Without them, your story would not be complete. For example, taking frequent breaks, slowing down, and receiving help are all adaptations people can report for low energy. Can you think of others? What about for symptoms such as loss of concentration, poor sleep, or memory loss? What are some adaptations people could make?

Think About Your Illness Before You Answer

Does your answer relate to your illness? If not, then think again; you may have given an irrelevant answer. Take for example, a common question on the Function Report: "Why did you stop working?" A client once wrote "poverty." Others have written homeless, domestic violence, taking care of children, and taking care of parents.

I understand how these matters can affect your job (or lack of one). I have had homeless clients who didn't have proper attire for interviews and worked with parents who couldn't find work due to childcare challenges. But these social and economic events are not covered by your disability insurance. If you must mention them, don't focus on them. What is our model definition of disability? An illness that affects your work and income. In the disability world, only medical causes get you on disability income.

Focus the Unfocused

If the question is broad and generic, bring it back to your illness. Broad and generic questions include: "What do you do throughout the day?" and "Describe what you do from the time you wake up until going to bed." Don't list only what you can do, which may make you look quite capable. Instead, explain how your illness has affected your daily activities, and how you have (or have not) adapted.

One of my clients loved cooking. Prior to his disability, he would make grand meals for family and friends. After his wife died, he fell into a deep depression and mostly ate alone. He didn't enjoy cooking anymore and made simple meals. These vivid details tell the story of depression. If he had simply listed "cooking" as one of his daily activities, he would have missed the chance to tell his story.

Be Concise
Again, no need to write a medical thriller. A few concise, relevant facts suffice. "I loved cooking. I used to make grand meals for family and friends. After my wife died and my depression began, I only make simple meals and eat alone."

Don't Be Embarrassed
Back in the early 2000s I had a client who suffered from disabling HIV. One day, he brought his Function Report to me for review. I thought the form was completed quite well, but I wondered why he downplayed his diarrhea. In previous conversations, he had described having explosive diarrhea in public. After the accidents, he carefully planned his route everywhere, including my office, so that he could access a bathroom anytime.

He admitted that he felt too embarrassed to write about the diarrhea, and didn't think he needed to, since the insurance company would review his medical records anyway. I told him that while the medical records did show "frequent diarrhea," they did not explain its impact on his life (e.g., restrictive traveling, can't be in public for long, etc.). By discussing the impact, he would explain his functional limitations.

Questions about our personal hygiene weigh on our dignity. We don't want to admit we can't take care of our bodies. But don't be embarrassed. There is nothing shameful. The body and the mind can get sick. Someday, they will perish. Don't let Lord Lizard shame you into hiding your symptoms and limitations. Be proud of the ways you have adapted and explain what help you still need. Express your limitations so that you can win your claim.

Think Beyond Can vs. Cannot

On the form, you will see questions that ask you: "Can you do A, B, C . . ." or "What can you do throughout the day?" But we know the truth is not so binary. When you see these "can you" questions, focus on the how instead.

Social interaction generates many "can you" questions. Can you spend time with others? Can you go to church? Can you meet with others regularly? Can you get along with people? Instead of quickly saying yes or no, report *how* your social life has changed since your disability began. For example, in reply to "Can you get along with others," instead of just saying yes or no, explain your situation: "I rarely interact with people because I isolate and don't go to social events. When I am with people I try not to engage."

Then there are good days and bad days. Maybe on good days you can spend more time with people, and on bad days less time with others. Describe on the form what happens on the bad days.

Transportation inspires many "can you" questions too. Can you drive? Can you take public transportation? Can you go out alone? Handle them as you would with other "can you" questions: by examining your daily activities and not rushing into conclusions. For example, "Can you drive?" might be answered with "I can only drive one hour a day. Driving creates anxiety that sometimes runs out of control."

Confirm Receipt

Make sure the Adjudicator receives your completed Function Report. If you cannot email the form, call them and let them know you have sent it to them, and ask for a receipt confirmation. And of course, if you have an attorney, let him submit it instead.

Share the completed form with your doctor and discuss your answers. It will help your doctor understand your disability better and help maintain consistency between the medical records and your answers on the Function Report.

CHAPTER 4

Getting to Know Your Maps

I have compared disability income systems to broken maps across America, "Think of the federal highway as Social Security benefits, the state road as State Disability benefits, and the county road as commercial disability insurance."

Traveling these roads can be lonely sometimes. This is probably your first trip, and you must travel alone, as your illness is yours alone and no one can suffer for you. Nevertheless, people who love you offer little gifts. Your family takes care of you, your friends bring laughter and hope. I offer to help you mend the broken maps.

In my Bountiful analogy, I categorized disability income by source (federal, state, commercial). Categorizing by source helps you compare the different systems. But to plan for disability, it is better to categorize by duration (Short-Term Disability vs. Long-Term Disability).

Generally, Short-Term Disability benefits can last a few months to a year, while Long-Term Disability benefits can continue as long as you are disabled, even until retirement.

The following chart compares the different types of disability income.

	Source	Duration
Employer Sponsored Short-Term Disability Insurance (STDI)	Commercial	Short-Term Disability
Employer Sponsored Long-Term Disability Insurance (LTDI)	Commercial	Long-Term Disability
State Disability	State	Short-Term Disability
Social Security Disability Insurance (SSDI)	Federal	Long-Term Disability

Can you tell which insurances are considered short term and which are long term? Yes, that's right, Employer Sponsored Short-Term Disability Insurance (STDI) and State Disability are considered short term. We will review these first. Some people call Short-Term Disability Insurance just STD. In this book, I will call it STDI.

Then we will visit Employer Sponsored Long-Term Disability Insurance (LTDI) and Social Security Disability Insurance (SSDI). These are the long-term insurances.

At the end of this chapter, we will review job and health insurance protections during your medical leave. Together, these three protections (income, job, health insurance) form your Triangle of Protections during your paid medical leave.

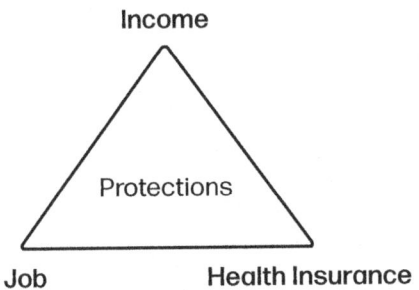

Short-Term Disability: Introduction/Lily's Story

Lily was a tour guide in San Francisco. When she found out I was a lawyer who helped people with disability, she told me her story. Two years earlier, she was on antidepressants. The medications made her too tired to climb hills. Well, if you can't climb hills, you can't show off San Francisco. I asked her if she applied for California State Disability.

She paused, blinked her eyes, and asked, "What's that?"

I wasn't surprised. Many disabled Californians don't know they have State Disability insurance. Instead, they apply for unemployment insurance. Besides being the wrong benefit (to get unemployment benefits you must be "willing, ready and able" to work, which you are not if you're too ill to work), unemployment insurance also pays only half of what State Disability generally pays.

"Well, that sucks. I wished I knew you back then. I really suffered."

"What's wrong with knowing me now?" I joked. "Did you file for unemployment?"

"No. Unfortunately."

"That's good, actually. That means you never claimed you were willing, ready, and able to work when you were actually disabled."

"But it has been so long. Did I miss the deadline?"

"Yes, you did miss the deadline, but we can file a good cause for late filing. I will help you."

"A good what?"

"Good cause for late filing. Meaning you had a good reason for not filing on time."

"What's the good reason?"

"You didn't know that it exists."

"Is that a legitimate reason?"

"Of course it is. Many people don't know they have State Disability. It is hard to find out when you are sick."

• • •

Short-Term Disability: State Disability

Lily ended up with a year's worth of State Disability back pay. The amount was so large it came in seven separate checks. Lily was lucky that the State of California accepted her good cause for late filing. They didn't have to, and she would have had to appeal her case and testify in front of a judge.

Like many Californian workers, Lily didn't know she had State Disability. So what is it? State Disability is a type of *Short-Term Disability* income. Some call it "temporary" disability. Five states and one US territory have State Disability:

- California
- Hawaii
- New York

- New Jersey
- Rhode Island
- Puerto Rico

I call them the Six Places. I would call them Six *Wonderful* Places if I didn't like to save words. Wonderful because workers there have Short-Term Disability protections.

State Disability is a hidden gem in the disability income world. Why hidden? Since its premium is *automatically* deducted from paychecks as a small tax (i.e., workers don't intentionally pay the petty amount), many workers don't know they have it.

I like State Disability because of its wide coverage. If you work as a W-2 employee in one of the Six Places, you most likely have it. You can confirm your State Disability coverage by asking your employer, since your employer deducts the State Disability tax from your paychecks.

I also like State Disability because it lasts a good length of time. In Hawaii, New York, New Jersey, and Puerto Rico, it lasts up to twenty-six weeks; in Rhode Island, thirty weeks; in California, it pays as long as fifty-two weeks! The following chart shows how long the State Disability benefits can last.

Jurisdiction	Maximum Benefit Period
CA	52 weeks
HI	26 weeks
NY	26 weeks
NJ	26 weeks
RI	30 weeks
PR	26 weeks

At twenty-six weeks minimum, they all last much longer than the standard FMLA break, which is up to twelve weeks per year. This means your State Disability can cover your entire FMLA medical leave and beyond if you need more time to rest and heal. (We will talk more about FMLA later.)

State Disability pays fairly well. Most State Disability programs pays at 60 percent to 70 percent of your wage; New Jersey pays as high as 85 percent. Since it may not be taxable, you may take home almost as much as your regular pay (but check with your accountant).

However, if you are a high earner, watch out for maximum benefit rate. For example, if you make $200K per year in California, California State Disability won't pay you 66 percent of $200K, or about $2500 a week. Instead, it will just pay you the maximum rate of $1,620 per week. That's because California State Disability only covers about $150,000 of your wage. If you earn much higher than $150,000/year, you want Employer Sponsored insurances, discussed next.

The following chart shows how much the various State Disability programs pay in 2023.

Jurisdiction	How Much It Pays	Maximum Weekly Benefit Amount
CA	66%	$1620
HI	58%	$765
NY	50%	$170
NJ	85%	$1025
RI	60%	$1007
PR	65%	$113

State Disability insurance can be run by either a government agency or a commercial insurer. When it is run by a government agency, it is called a State Plan. Most people with State Disability have the State Plan. The rest are commercially insured, and those commercial policies must provide equal or better terms than the State Plan. In this book, any insurance used to satisfy the state requirement for Short-Term Disability is considered State Disability, whether it is run by corporations or government.

Some workers mistake State Disability for welfare because a government agency processes and pays the claims. They shy away from it because they don't want welfare money. It is not welfare. The workers have paid into the system, they just don't know it.

To qualify for State Disability, you must have a serious illness that disables you from your *current/most recent* job. Not *any or all* jobs, just your most recent job. Review Part One if you are unsure whether you are "disabled enough" to apply.

I talk about the six State Disability programs together, but they are not managed by one overarching entity. Each state has its own program, and each program follows its own state regulations. Yes, just like DMVs.

• • •

Short-Term Disability: Employer Sponsored Short-Term Disability Insurance (STDI)

The Six Places are wonderful, but what if you don't work there? How would you get temporary disability income?

If you are lucky, you have STDI. Employer Sponsored means the insurance is provided through your employer *voluntarily*. It is distinct from State Disability, which is required by law. Most employers don't sponsor STDI, so don't be surprised if you don't have it. But when employers do offer it, it is an awesome benefit.

In my broken map analogy, I compared Employer Sponsored policies to county roads. That's because they have the smallest reach. Federal benefits transverse the United States, and state benefits reach the state borders, but Employer Sponsored policies only cover employees within a company.

Great highways all look the same, but little county roads twist and turn around the countryside in their own special ways. Similarly, Employer Sponsored policies vary greatly from company to company. Below are general observations; always check your policies to confirm what applies to you.

Attorneys who work on Employer Sponsored benefits are called ERISA attorneys. ERISA stands for Employee Retirement Income Security Act, a federal law that regulates employee benefits. The law doesn't require employers to provide disability insurance, but if they do, they must comply with ERISA (exceptions exist for some governmental or religious employers. When in doubt, check with an ERISA attorney).

Checking for Employer Sponsored disability coverage

According to the Department of Labor's statistics, the bigger the company, the more likely it will sponsor disability insurance. The higher your wage, the more likely you have Employer Sponsored disability coverage.

To see if you have STDI coverage, you can (of course) ask your employer. But sometimes it is not so easy. Workers may not want their employer to know about their possible disability. Others fear discrimination. So here are other ways to check.

Check your employer's benefits web page or the employee handbook. It should give you basic information like which classes of employees are entitled to STDI coverage, how much it pays, and for how long.

Check your paystubs. If disability insurance premiums are deducted from your paychecks, the deductions should appear on your paystubs.

• • •

In STDI, disability is defined as the inability to substantially complete one's current or most recent job due to a serious illness (just like in State Disability). *Not any job, just the current or most recent job* (just like in State Disability). I re-emphasize this point because many people think that in order to get a short paid medical leave, they must be disabled from all jobs.

The average maximum benefit period is twenty-six weeks, according to the US Department of Labor. But some policies last as little as twelve weeks. Use the maximum benefit period to help you plan for disability. Do you think you can go back within the maximum benefit period? If not, you should consider Long-Term Disability.

STDI usually pays about 2/3 of your salary, capped at a certain amount. If you have both State Disability and STDI, watch out for subrogation. Subrogation means your STDI benefit is reduced dollar for dollar by any other disability income, such as State Disability. For example, let's say you work in Hawaii and you get STDI benefit at $1,650/week. Your Hawaiian State Disability pays you $650/week. Under Subrogation, you will need to return $650/week benefit to the STDI insurer. You are only entitled to $1,000 from STDI. Subrogation prevents double dipping.

Employer Sponsored policies are mostly administered by commercial insurers, but they can also be administered by a third-party administrator, sometimes called an absence management company. When you make a disability claim, you make it to the administrator.

Some Employer Sponsored disability insurances are self-insured or self-funded. In these plans, it is the employer, not an insurance company, that pays the disability benefits. Nevertheless, these plans usually hire an insurance company or third-party administrator to process the disability claims of their employees.

• • •

What if you have neither State Disability nor Employer Sponsored Short-Term Disability?

If you are not seriously ill, try buying Individual Insurance from a broker or insurance company. Individual Insurance, also known as individual policy, is a contract between two private parties: the Commercial Insurance company and the insured (you). It contrasts with Group Insurance, which you get as part of a group of people, like fellow employees in your company. Small business owners and 1099 independent contractors often have Individual Insurance to manage risk of disability; W-2 employees usually don't. If you are seriously ill, you are unlikely to secure Individual Insurance.

If you are injured at work, you should consider worker's compensation. If you are not sure whether your illness/injury is work related, talk to a worker's compensation attorney immediately.

Another possible source of income is Paid Family Medical Leave (PFML). Like State Disability, PFML is mandated by the state. Unlike State Disability, you don't have to be disabled to get it, but you do have to be seriously ill. It exists in the following jurisdictions: Washington, Connecticut, Massachusetts, District of Columbia, Oregon, Colorado (in 2024) and Delaware (in 2026).

Don't confuse PFMLs with the federal Family Medical Leave Act (FMLA). The federal FMLA protects your job and health insurance, but *not* income. On the other hand, all PFMLs protect income. In Massachusetts, Oregon, and Washington, PFMLs protect job and health insurance as well.

A drawback of the PFMLs is the very short period of benefits, shorter than all State Disability programs. Think of PFML as a disability-lite benefit. Massachusetts offers twenty weeks of paid medical leave, Washington, Connecticut, and Oregon offer twelve weeks, and the District of Columbia offers only six weeks.

Also check to see if your employer has an internal policy to provide paid medical leave beyond the accrued sick or PTO hours. It doesn't hurt to ask. And you can always negotiate with your employer for advanced pay.

Don't forget to consider all possible sources of accident-related insurance, such as auto, travel, accidental death and dismemberment (AD&D), and financial critical illness. These benefits are not as robust as disability benefits, but they can provide some financial assistance.

Some people get on unemployment insurance, even though they are not supposed to (it requires someone to be ready, willing, and able to work). Nevertheless, unemployment benefits remain the last defense against pennilessness for many ill Americans. County assistance pays little, if any.

• • •

Summary

- Short-Term Disability income replaces lost wages for a short time, like six months.

- There are two major types of Short-Term Disability income: State Disability and Employer Sponsored Short-Term Disability Insurance (STDI).
- State Disability is required in California, Hawaii, New York, New Jersey, Rhode Island, and Puerto Rico.
- STDI is offered through the employer as a Group Insurance.
- Short-Term Disability replaces about 2/3 of your wage, capped at a certain amount.
- PFML provides income protection and is available in Connecticut, Massachusetts, Washington, Oregon, and the District of Columbia.

Long-Term Disability: Introduction

Here is our friendly chart again. Can you find the two types of Long-Term Disability insurance?

	Source	Duration
Employer Sponsored Short-Term Disability Insurance (STDI)	Commercial	Short-Term Disability
Employer Sponsored Long-Term Disability Insurance (LTDI)	Commercial	Long-Term Disability
State Disability	State	Short-Term Disability
Social Security Disability Insurance (SSDI)	Federal	Long-Term Disability

恭喜! This means Congratulations! in Cantonese, pronounced gong hei. You got them right! The two types of Long-Term Disability protections are:

1. LTDI
2. SSDI

When you are on Short-Term Disability, you should decide whether to apply for Long-Term Disability benefits.

Long-Term Disability: Long-Term Disability Insurance (LTDI)

You have met STDI, the little cousin of LTDI. They belong to the same family of Employer Sponsored policies, so they share many similarities. In our Bountiful analogy, they are like unique county roads, varying greatly from company to company (countryside to countryside). As such, below are generalizations. Always check your policies to confirm what applies to you.

You can check whether you have LTDI the same way you check for STDI, as described above. Don't be surprised if you don't have LTDI coverage. According to the Department of Labor, only one-third of US workers have LTDI coverage. Just like its shorter cousin (STDI), the bigger your company, the more likely you have LTDI coverage. The higher your income, the more likely you have LTDI coverage.

Like STDI, LTDI usually pays about two-thirds of your income. Income is determined by looking at your most recent salary (usually within the last two years). It may not include commission, bonuses, and overtime pay. Check your policy to see exactly how it is calculated.

Just like STDI, there is subrogation. Most LTDI will offset for State Disability and Social Security benefits, dollar for dollar. There is also an offset for worker's compensation. If the combination of your disability income is higher than your regular wage, you may owe money to one of the insurers.

LTDIs may last as long as you remain disabled and until your retirement age. Because the benefit period can last so long, insurers continue to scrutinize LTDI claims after approval, trying to find ways to deny it and stop benefits.

LTDIs have Waiting Periods around three to six months. During the Waiting Period, you are not eligible for LTDI benefits, and should be getting income from STDI, State Disability, or accrued sick time instead. If your employer offers both STDI and LTDI, the STDI should last through the Waiting Period of the LTDI to give you seamless income. The Waiting Period is often called the elimination period in the Commercial Insurance world.

Generally, during the *first two years of disability*, disability is defined as the inability to perform your *current/most recent* job. After the first two years, disability is defined as the inability to perform *any or most* job, befitting your educational and vocational backgrounds. This "any job" definition distinguishes LTDI from STDI and State Disability, which only use the "current/most recent" job standard.

Most LTDIs limit benefits on mental illness claims to two years. These illnesses are considered self-reported, solely based on the claimant's words. There is little, if any, objective testing for them. Because of the lack of objective evidence, mental illnesses are often treated with suspicion. If you can prove additional disabling physical illness, your benefits may continue beyond the two years. Switching your claim from "mental" to "physical" can be tricky, so ask an ERISA lawyer to help you.

Like STDIs, LTDIs are mostly administered by Commercial Insurance companies, but they can also be administered by a third-party administrator, sometimes called an absence management company. And like STDI, LTDIs can be self-insured.

Your employer (and its human resources department) may provide some basic information on how to apply for LTDI, but do not expect them to advocate for you. This is natural. If you are claiming Long-Term Disability, your relationship with the employer can turn tenuous. You may not ever return to your job. This is where many employees get frustrated with the disability process. They feel their employer is not helping them, which is true.

After getting approved, maintain your claim. Continue to see your doctor, follow treatment, answer the insurer's correspondence, etc. The insurer may want to know if you can work part time (so they can pay you less). Some insurers send private investigators to monitor the insured. You can easily Google this and find some harrowing stories. Bottom line: Do not expect your LTDI to continue without maintenance. Getting approved is a step toward securing your finances, not the last.

• • •

Long-Term Disability: Social Security Disability Insurance (SSDI)

Taxes are deducted from your paychecks, and they seem to go nowhere and be forever lost. But if you become disabled, you will be glad to know you have been paying Social Security tax.

Unlike LTDI, which covers mostly workers with higher socioeconomic statuses, SSDI covers almost all US workers. For many, it is the only Long-Term Disability protection.

SSDI is a strange animal with many undesirable features. But it comes with a golden horn: health insurance. After twenty-four months of SSDI payments, you will be entitled to Medicare. Some SSDI recipients may easily access Medicaid based on financial needs.

If you don't qualify for SSDI, you may qualify for SSI. The Social Security Administration (SSA) runs two disability programs: Social Security Disability Insurance (SSDI) and Supplemental Security Income (SSI). The SSI program is for people with limited work history and financial resources, so don't let a lack of work history dissuade you from applying for federal benefits. If you need help, apply. Some workers get both SSDI and SSI when their SSDI benefit amount is too low.

How much you get on SSDI ("SSDI rate") depends on your work history. The easiest way to find your SSDI rate is by accessing your online account at the SSA: https://www.ssa.gov/myaccount/. Alternatively, you can call Social Security at (800) 772-1213 or visit a local office (be prepared to wait). The average monthly SSDI rate in 2023 is around $1,483. The maximum rate is about $3,600.

After approval, SSDI pays as long as you are disabled or until your retirement. Periodically, your case will be medically reviewed to determine whether you are still disabled. SSDI is more stable than LTDI because SSDI is not as aggressive as LTDI in cutting off benefits. Generally, Social Security performs a medical review every few years.

• • •

How does SSDI define disability?

Social Security has a unique definition of disability. It defines disability as the inability to perform Substantial Gainful Activities (SGA) due to a medical condition that would likely last for twelve months or more or result in death.

Here is a triangle to help you remember the definition of disability under Social Security.

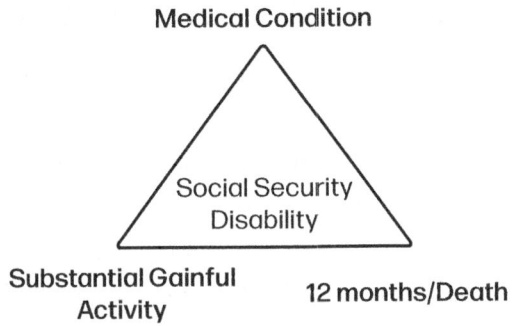

Practically speaking, you should consider applying for Social Security disability if you are in any of these situations:

- You have been disabled for twelve months or more,
- You are likely to be disabled for twelve months or more, or
- You are diagnosed with a terminal disease.

What is Substantial Gainful Activity (SGA)?

SGA means a certain level of work activities. Social Security defines SGA by a dollar amount, so it is easy to know if you are earning SGA or above. Here is the SGA dollar amount per month from 2017 to 2023:

Year	Nonblind ($)	Blind ($)
2017	1170	1950
2018	1180	1970
2019	1220	2040
2020	1260	2110
2021	1310	2190
2022	1350	2260
2023	1470	2460

One set of the SGA amount is for people with blindness, the other for people with sight. For example, for a nonblind individual, the SGA amount in 2020 is $1,260/mo. That means that if a person is making $1,260 or more per month, he is making SGA. If he is making SGA, then he can't be disabled under Social Security. Exceptions exist. If you are disabled but making SGA or above, consult a Social Security attorney before you apply.

Notice the SGA is a low amount. You don't have to make much money to cross the line. Also, the SGA can be from any job, not just the claimant's customary job. These two features make Social Security's definition of disability harder to satisfy.

If you are self-employed, Social Security also wants to know how much effort you put into your work. If your efforts match a regular full-time worker, you may have SGA, even if you have no profit. Social Security uses three clumsy tests for self-employed applicants. If you suspect that your self-employment is SGA, consult a Social Security attorney.

What is the application deadline for Social Security disability?

There is no deadline per se, but if you wait too long to apply, you may lose retroactive benefits. Retroactive benefit (back pay) for SSDI is limited to twelve months of benefits prior to your application date.

Also, if you wait a long time to apply, your doctors may not be available to vouch for you. They may have retired or moved elsewhere. Your medical records become old and hard to find, making it difficult to prove your disability.

If you have both LTDI and SSDI coverage, focus on getting your LTDI approved at the start of your disability. First, the LTDI probably pays much more than the SSDI. Second, due to subrogation, most of your SSDI will go to the commercial insurer anyway. Third, your LTDI has a stricter application deadline than your SSDI. But that doesn't mean you should forget about SSDI. Remember, SSDI is more stable than LTDI and comes with Medicare.

How do you know if you are financially qualified to apply for SSI?

Practically speaking, you don't have to figure that out on your own. When you apply for disability, the SSA will help you apply for both, unless you actively tell them you don't want SSI.

To qualify for SSI, you cannot have resources over $2,000. Generally, things you can easily sell for cash are considered "resources." However, the home you live in, and one car are exempt from being counted as resources. If you are denied because you are over the resource limit, do not give away money and properties so that you qualify for SSI. This can backfire and make you ineligible for SSI in the future. You should talk to a Social Security attorney to see how you can properly spend-down your resources.

People who are financially eligible for SSI are considered vulnerable populations; therefore, many local governments and nonprofit organizations provide services to help them get on disability. If you think you qualify for SSI, try to access SSI advocacy from the local county government, your public health clinic, or a legal aid office within your local area.

Are immigrants eligible for SSDI or SSI?

Some documented immigrants are eligible for SSDI, SSI, or both. The rules regarding Social Security and immigration are complicated, but a good place to learn about these rules is the National Immigration Law Center (www.nilc.org). Connect with your local legal aid office to find out if you are eligible.

Some immigrants are not eligible for SSI due to their immigration status. However, some local governments step up and provide benefits instead. For example, in California, some documented immigrants who would qualify for SSI but for their immigration status can receive income from Cash Assistance Program for Immigrants (CAPI).

• • •

Summary

- LTDI is a Commercial Insurance through the employer. To qualify, the disability must last longer than the Waiting Period. The Waiting Period is usually six months.
- SSDI is a disability insurance through the federal government. It is for people who are disabled for at least twelve months.

- SSDI comes with Medicare.
- People who do not qualify for SSDI may get SSI instead.
- Some documented immigrants are eligible for SSDI, SSI, or both.

• • •

We have finished discussing your income protection. Before we talk about job and health insurance protections, let's hear a story.

Han's Story

Han was a petite Chinese woman who survived the Cambodian genocide. She came to my office with her social worker, Jake Chang.

"The soldiers clubbed my little brother to death," she whispered to me in Mandarin. "They didn't shoot him because they didn't want to waste a bullet. He was too little to work, worthless to their revolution."

Jake handed me Han's medical records. He didn't want Han to relive her trauma so I read it instead.

After coming to the US as a refugee, Han worked in restaurants and factories in the Bay Area. A nonprofit mental health clinic in San Francisco treated her PTSD and depression. Her mental health had always been poor, but in the early 2000s, it deteriorated. Her nightmares resurfaced. She dreamed of people eating babies. She startled easily, almost pouring boiling water on a coworker when a couple of young men walked into the shop unexpectedly. She suspected her boss and coworkers were afraid of her. Her emotions rotated from anger to sadness to despair, but she couldn't tell anyone why.

Her psychiatrist upped her psych meds, which suppressed the dreams but also dulled her. One day at home, she lost focus, fell down the stairs, and hurt her arm. Her housemate brought her to the hospital.

After her discharge, Han couldn't go back to her job. Jake helped her apply for Social Security disability. The claim was denied.

"What went wrong, Andy?" Jake asked in English. "Did I do anything wrong?"

"I would need to see her Social Security file." I answered.

"How long would that take? Han is running out of money to pay for rent."

"A few days," I said. "But why is she not on State Disability?"

Silence. Jake had forgotten that immigrants pay into California State Disability just like any other worker. I immediately helped Han apply.

A few days later, Han's file arrived. I learned that the SSA was investigating Han for fraud. They thought she was faking her symptoms to get government benefits. Several years ago, she saw a therapist in Oakland who was linked with a series of welfare frauds. Although no longer a patient of that therapist, Han was blacklisted by the SSA. What made this Oakland therapist so infamous? I called my friend Sam at Bay Area Legal Aid (BALA) to find out. Sam worked at BALA's Oakland office and managed their Social Security Advocacy program.

The whole thing started with a grant, Sam explained. The therapist was a PTSD specialist and had received a private foundation grant to help Cambodian refugees. When her patients became disabled with PTSD, she helped them apply for disability. After a while, Social Security became suspicious. How could every one of her patients be a PTSD survivor? And why were they all Cambodians? The SSA suspected that the therapist was a Cambodian insider conspiring with the Cambodian community to defraud the United States government.

A few months later, Han came to thank me. Her Social Security appeal was still pending, but her State Disability had been approved. She had money to live. She expected to be well soon and asked me to drop her Social Security claim.

"America has been good to me," she said. "It gave me a home, a refuge. I don't want to take any more from others. I will go back to work soon."

I asked if she knew both of her State Disability and Social Security Disability Insurance are insurance. She had paid for the insurance premium in the form of taxes. She had no idea.

"You are not taking anything from anyone." I assured her. "It is your right. You paid for it. This is not free money. It is insurance. If you were in a car accident, would you hesitate to claim your car insurance?"

"My sister told me I can't become a citizen if I ever get on welfare."

"Your sister is confusing disability insurance with SSI [Supplemental Security Income]. Sometimes SSI affects people getting permanent residency, which you already have. Again, Social Security Disability Insurance and State Disability, the benefits you applied for, are not welfare."

She nodded. I asked if she was feeling better.

She said yes and showed me her arm. "It's healed. But I still have nightmares, although not as much. A few days ago, I even had a new flashback. A mosquito buzzed over my ear, and I panicked, I didn't know why. I sat down, took deep breaths, and pictured a happy face like Mr. Chang taught me. That night I dreamed of my little brother. He looked radiant. He said he was not angry anymore and I shouldn't be either. He told me to look behind him, and I saw a murky lake swarming with mosquitos. I woke up crying, remembering that's where the soldiers took him away from us."

"A breakthrough?" I tried to sound positive.

"Yes, it was. I was afraid that not working and staying at home would make me crazy, but I do feel better. I even called some relatives. My psychiatrist lowered my medications. Oh, and I started gardening."

She took out a bouquet of hyacinths from a Safeway paper bag.

"These are for you, Andy! Please accept them. I didn't buy them from Safeway, it is just a bag. Can you believe I grew all these beautiful flowers?"

・・・

Job and Health Insurance Protections

On the road ahead you will get sick of me warning you: *Don't quit your job!* At least don't quit without deliberation. Once you quit your job, you lose many employee rights. Instead of quitting, invoke your legal rights to medical leave. Yes, even Midas needs a break. Here, I show you how.

Family Medical Leave Act (FMLA)

The FMLA is the mother of all job protections. It is a federal law that protects you when you take time off for your health. Under FMLA, you can take up to twelve weeks of FMLA leave every twelve months.

During the twelve-week leave, your employer must maintain your group health insurance. So, while your job is protected, so is your health insurance. After the twelve weeks, you are entitled to return to the same or comparable job at your employer.

The leave can be for your own serious illness (the subject of this book) or to take care of a family member who is seriously ill (not the subject of this book). Notice FMLA doesn't require a disability status, "serious illness" is enough.

What is serious? The term "serious" is broadly defined under FMLA. If your illness requires inpatient care or continuous outpatient treatments (e.g., weekly psychotherapy), it is most likely serious.

The FMLA does not provide income (except during an emergency like COVID). That's why you should get disability income or PFML. Otherwise, your medical leave would be *unpaid*.

The FMLA prevents the employer from firing you for taking a break, but it doesn't protect you from being fired for "legitimate" reasons. For example, your employer downsizes and fires all employees in your job classification. You and your peers are fired. Sometimes it is hard to tell if you are fired for legitimate reasons. If you are fired during your leave, consult an employment attorney.

Not all employers are required to offer FMLA leaves. An employer who must comply with FMLA is called a covered employer. Ask your employer if it is a covered employer under FMLA. If it has fifty employees or more, it is probably a covered employer.

Not all employees are eligible to take FMLA leaves. One eligibility requirement is having worked 1,250 hours during the twelve months prior to the start of leave. Therefore, brand-new employees may not be eligible.

State Job Protections: State FMLA and PFML

There are also state versions of FMLA, which can offer employees even more protections. For example, California's FMLA is called California Family Right Act (CFRA). It covers employers with five or more employees. If you are not entitled to federal FMLA leave, see if you qualify for any state FMLA leave. To learn more, Google "FMLA" plus the name of your state.

Paid Family Medical Leave (PFML) in Massachusetts, Oregon, and Washington State provide job and health insurance protections. PFML in DC and Connecticut do not.

If you don't qualify for leave under state or federal protections, then your other option is to ask for a leave of absence under the company's policy. If they do not grant you the leave of absence, check with an employment attorney for any disability discrimination.

Job Protection Is Not Necessarily Income Protection

Don't confuse income protections with job/health insurance protections. Don't assume that if your disability income is approved, then your job is simultaneously secured, or vice versa. Always check with your employer to see if you need to apply for them separately.

Maintaining Health Insurance

Your job is protected under FMLA, as is your health insurance. However, you still need to maintain your health insurance. Why maintain? Usually, an employee's contribution to their health insurance premium comes from a payroll deduction. But if you are not on payroll because you are receiving disability income instead of wages, you may have to actively pay for your own premium in order to maintain the health insurance. Ask your employer about how to maintain your health insurance during your leave. Who pays for the premium? You or the employer? Who is the payee? When is it due? You don't want to lose your health insurance during your medical break.

If you don't return to your employer after your medical leave, you will need to look for health insurance. The federal law Consolidated Omnibus Budget Reconciliation Act (COBRA) allows you and your dependents to continue the same health insurance that you have through your employer for up to eighteen months.

Alternatively, you can buy your own health insurance from an insurance broker/agent or visit your state's health insurance online marketplace. These online marketplaces were created under the Affordable Care Act (ACA), which some people call Obamacare. Buying health insurance from these marketplaces can possibly save you money due to a federal subsidy. Not all states have an ACA marketplace. Find out about your state at www.healthcare.gov/marketplace-in-your-state/.

• • •

Summary
- The federal FMLA protects your job for up to twelve weeks when you take time off for medical reasons.
- Some states have their own version of FMLA that provide similar or additional protections.
- Some PFML laws provide job and health insurance protections.
- When your job is protected by FMLA, so is your health insurance from your employer.
- During your paid medical leave, you may have to make the premium payments to maintain your health insurance.

CHAPTER 5

Seven Steps to Your Paid Medical Leave: Introduction

You may remember how taking a paid medical leave saved Mary, my designer client. You may also remember how the leave may prevent a *disability crisis*. And now that you have learned about the different disability protections, let's integrate them and learn how to take a three-month paid medical leave.

A paid medical leave gives you the option of returning to your job afterward. During the leave, your wage is replaced by either disability insurance or Paid Family Medical Leave (PFML). Your health insurance stays the same due to state and federal protections.

Charles Mujie, cofounder of nimsa, compares paid medical leave to time out during a game. When you call time out during a game, you stop the clock. You take a break from running after goals; you don't get penalized if you make a mistake. Instead, you rest, regroup, and recharge. Charles recognized that a paid medical leave offers the same benefits in a career. When you take a paid medical leave, you don't get written up for poor performance at work. You don't get demoted or fired for not hitting goals. Instead, you rest and heal.

Taking a paid medical leave can save your life. It can save your health, career, relationship, and your sanity. It deters a disability crisis. You free yourself from work: the unforgiving schedule, the daily grind, the goals, and the personalities of workplace. You focus on your health and well-being instead.

Three months is the default period for a paid medical leave, because FMLA generally protects your job up to three months. At the end of the leave, you can return to the same job, but you don't have to. You have other options. You can choose to move on to another job, perhaps one that's a better fit for your health.

Dawn Gross, MD, (co-founder of Dyalogues and ICU for the Soul) regards the income, job, and health insurance benefits as a dome of protections. When you are in the dome, or "Triangle of Protections" as I call it, you can safely explore your options.

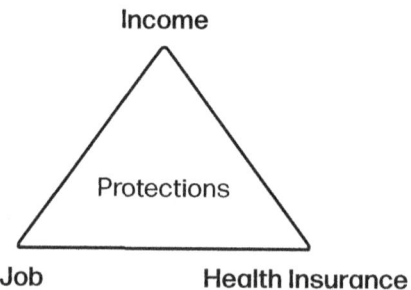

The following is a list of seven steps to getting a three-month paid medical leave. The list is general. It doesn't cover every situation possible. It doesn't include everything you need to do; it may contain things inapplicable to you. You may have benefits or

SEVEN STEPS TO YOUR PAID MEDICAL LEAVE: INTRODUCTION

protections beyond the scope of this list. Exceptions may apply to your situation. Use this list to help you explore your options, not dictate your actions. There is no guarantee that your disability claim or medical leave will be approved by following this list. No one can guarantee that. The list is roughly in the order of things you should do. But reality is messy. Traveler, feel free to adjust your itinerary as you see fit.

- Step One: Start Your Healing Journey with a Supportive Doctor
- Step Two: Get to Know Your Protections
- Step Three: Decide on a Date Last Work (DLW)
- Step Four: Apply for Job and Health Insurance Protections
- Step Five: Apply for Disability Benefits
- Step Six: Rest, Heal, and Maintain Your Benefits
- Step Seven: Consider Your Future

Step One: Start Your Healing Journey with a Supportive Doctor

Start by acknowledging your emotions. Write them in a journal. Are you psychologically stuck somewhere, like we talked about in Chapter 2? Becoming aware is the beginning of healing. When you are ready, express those feelings to your doctor. Tell her everything. All the despair, anxiety, fear, confusion, depression; let it all out. Revisit Chapter 3 for tips on how to help your doctor understand your disability.

Whether you have been in mental health treatment for a day or a lifetime, commit or recommit to healing. Don't waver, don't give up. Regardless of how hard life seems, maintain your treatment. See a mental health specialist. Take your medication. Meditate.

Exercise. Eat well. Connect with loved ones. Ignore Lord Lizard. Do these things for your mental health, not for claiming disability. You may not even need disability benefits if you heal quickly. Maybe all you need is a month off in Hawaii.

But if you are not getting better and falling behind at work, find the right time to bring up disability with your doctor. The right time can be a few days, a few months, or a few years from now. No one can tell you what to do. Look at your life. How severe is your mental illness? Do you have a trusting relationship with your doctor? Have you been reporting your symptoms and limitations to your doctor? Have you found a psychotherapist? Where do you see yourself in six months if you don't take a medical leave? Are you secretly asking too many "Can I" questions?

The right time to talk is not always the right time to decide. Bring it up and see how your doctor responds. Most of the time, doctors are supportive. But if your doctor is not, give her some time. Sometimes she is just surprised. She has never heard you talk about disability, and she is confused. If you suddenly begin to report your symptoms (perhaps due to practicing the knowledge from this book), it can be disorienting for the doctor. Help the doctor understand your disability.

Some doctors may refuse you out of misguided care. They don't want you to "be" disabled, "feel" disabled, and rely on disability income, as though it is an addictive substance like opiates. To address their concern tell them that without income, you can't pay bills, which will surely worsen your health.

If your doctor doesn't want to put you on "permanent disability," explain Short-Term Disability to her. And tell her that you have a great cheerleader—the insurers—on your side to get you back

SEVEN STEPS TO YOUR PAID MEDICAL LEAVE: INTRODUCTION

to work. They will stop your benefit and get you back to work as soon as you (and they) can!

Other doctors simply have not known you long enough. Most doctors don't want to be known as the "go to" doctor to fill out disability forms in the community. They want to establish long and trusting relationships with their patients (just as you do). This is normal and reasonable. If you are working with a new doctor, ask your doctor if she is willing to support you incrementally.

For example, ask her to certify you for just a couple of months, and agree to revisit the issue on a set date. Your new doctor may find this baby-step approach more palatable. Or ask the doctor when she can decide whether to support you. In my experience, there is no set time. Some doctors want six months to observe, other doctors want three visits.

Although rare, there are doctors who may never be supportive of you, unless you are extremely debilitated, like being in a coma. But in those extreme cases, you don't need their support anyway. These doctors can be quite demanding of their patients. One time, a young doctor told me that none of his patients would ever need disability protections while under his care. He expected all of his patients to be well and act well. Oh boy, was he quickly surprised.

Ultimately, you want to be under the care of a doctor that meets you where you are, not the other way around. It is okay to switch doctors when the relationship is no longer supportive and constructive. If your doctor makes you feel guilty or shameful about applying for disability, then you may need another doctor.

If you can, get treatment from a psychotherapist. Normally, providers are good at documenting symptoms, but not so good at documenting limitations of daily living. But therapists are good at doing both, probably because the nature of psychotherapy is to help one cope with everyday life. Remember, for disability claims, we need both symptoms and functional limitations.

When you are with your primary care doctor or orthopedic surgeon, you don't usually have fifty minutes to just talk about life. But with a therapist, you do. The extra time can help you lay a solid foundation for your disability claim. If your psychotherapist has the right credentials (e.g., MD, PhD, PsyD), they can even certify your disability claim.

Step Two: Get to Know Your Protections

While you are seeing your doctor and therapist about your mental health, consistently reporting your symptoms and limitations, start learning your legal and insurance protections. Maybe you will never use them. That's okay. At least get to know them, so you know how to protect yourself, in case you need them.

The Triangle of Protections reminds us of what to protect during a paid medical leave: income, job, and health insurance.

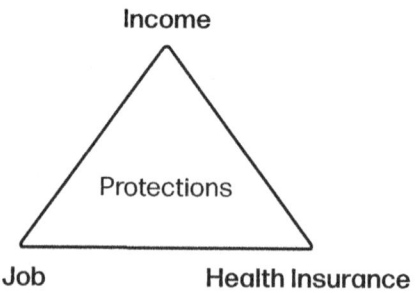

First, let's start with income. If you don't work for three months, how will you get income? Your first line of defense is your

SEVEN STEPS TO YOUR PAID MEDICAL LEAVE: INTRODUCTION

Short-Term Disability insurances. Complete the chart below for an overview of your short-term income protections.

	STDI	State Disability
Do you have it?		
How much does it pay?		
For up to how long?		
Waiting Period		

In STDI and State Disability, the Waiting Period is usually seven to fourteen days of disability. Sometimes the Waiting Period is called the elimination period. During this period, you are not eligible for disability income (exceptions exist: for example, you work in Rhode Island). Your disability benefit begins the day after your Waiting Period. During the Waiting Period, get paid using your Paid Time Off (PTO), accrued vacation or sick hours.

If you work in District of Colombia, Connecticut, Oregon, Massachusetts, and Washington State, see if you qualify for income under Paid Family Medical Leave (PFML).

Find out how to apply. If you have a State Plan, you can probably apply on a state agency's website. If you have Employer Sponsored disability insurance, you will apply to a Commercial Insurance carrier or a third-party administrator.

Be aware of *when* you can apply and the application deadlines. Some insurers require you to apply *after* your waiting/elimination period is over, like California State Disability, while others allow you to start applying before you stop working. State Disability, PFML and ERISA claims have strict deadlines. Be sure to mark them in your calender.

Identify exclusions on your disability insurance. Does a pre-existing condition disqualify you? Is your illness work related and therefore excluded from coverage? If yes, talk to a lawyer before you apply.

Find out if your employer can *integrate* your disability benefits with accrued sick/vacation hours or Paid Time Off (PTO). Most disability insurance replaces up to two-thirds of your income. You can use your accrued sick and vacation hours, or PTO, to make up the difference, so that you get close to 100 percent of your regular income.

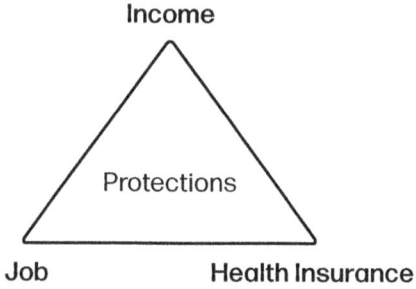

Now, let's look at job and health insurance. If you stop working without getting an approval on your medical leave, you may lose your job. To get job protection, find out if the federal FMLA applies to your employer. This should be easy, as most employers (and their human resources departments) know whether they must comply with FMLA. It is a big deal to them.

Find out how much FMLA leave you are entitled to take. If you are not a new employee and you haven't used FMLA within the last twelve months, you should be able to take up to twelve weeks.

Find out how to apply for FMLA leave. Your employer may ask you and your doctor to complete a form. Under FMLA, you and your doctor do not have to reveal details of your illness. If you employer pries into your medical privacy, contact an employment lawyer.

If the federal FMLA doesn't apply to you, check to see if you are entitled to your state's FMLA or PFML, or request a leave under your employer's internal policy.

Get details on how your health insurance will be paid during your break. Are you paying the premium? Or is the employer? What is the amount? Where do you send the payment?

At this stage, you're dealing frequently with your employer's human resources department. Keep in mind where their loyalty lies and who they work for. This will save you a lot of heartaches.

When my aunt became disabled, she expected her human resources department to guide her through the disability claim process. After all, it was an *Employer Sponsored* benefit. She was disappointed. The employer (and its human resources department) only has to meet certain legal standards. Its business is not to provide benefits counseling to you. Think health insurance: while you get health insurance through your employer, you wouldn't expect your employer to secure medical treatments for you.

Bottom line: Do not expect much of what the employer can and will do for you. Remember, your disability is the antithesis of what a company stands for—production. You are responsible for planning and claiming your own disability benefits.

Step Three: Decide on a Date Last Work (DLW)

Your supportive biographers (doctor and psychotherapist) have been writing about you (in your medical records). You have researched your legal and insurance protections and know how much time you can take off. Now, talk to your doctor and agree on the Date Last Work (DLW). It is the last date you will work before your paid medical leave. After this date, your leave begins.

If you have already stopped working due to a medical reason, you don't have to plan a DLW, as it has already happened. For example, you were hospitalized for panic attacks two weeks ago and you haven't worked since. The last date you worked prior to the attack is your DLW. If you have already passed your Waiting Period, you are eligible to apply for disability income.

Talk to your family members about your DLW, if you haven't already. How will life change for you and your family after your DLW? Any changes in routine? What support do you need from them?

Continue to see your doctors to establish medical evidence for your disability.

Step Four: Apply for Job and Health Insurance Protections

Once you have confirmed the Date Last Work (DLW) with your doctor, ask for a medical leave from your employer, using federal or state FMLA. When your job is protected, so is your health insurance, meaning you keep your group health insurance through your employer. If your employer is not bound by any FMLA laws, apply for a leave under the employer's internal policy.

The federal FMLA states that you should ask for the medical leave at least thirty days before your leave, but that's not always possible. Circumstances change. Illness can suddenly deteriorate. Notify your employer as soon as you know you want the medical leave.

Your employer will likely ask you to complete a form for the leave. The form is usually straightforward. Expect some back and forth between you and the employer, as the process is "interactive."

If the employer denies your request for FMLA, *don't quit!* Unfortunately, many workers despair and quickly give up when the employer rejects their FMLA request. Instead of taking a paid medical leave where their job and health insurances are protected, they quit their job. This can be a detrimental move. Not only do they lose their job security, but they also lose their health insurance. Furthermore, once they quit, their Employer Sponsored disability claim gets messy. Remember Daniel? Instead of quitting, contact an employment lawyer.

Stop working immediately after your Date Last Work. Don't confuse "stop working" with "quitting your job." *You are not quitting your job!* You are still an employee of your employer; the employment relationship gives you the rights to many disability benefits. Don't give them up so easily.

Step Five: Apply for Disability Benefits

Notify your employer that you want to apply for Short-Term Disability income. You may apply for either Employer Sponsored Short-Term Disability Insurance (STDI) or State Disability benefits. Yes, you can apply for both if you have both. Watch out for subrogation. If you work in a state with Paid Family Medical Leave (PFML), apply for PFML instead of State Disability.

Be explicit to your employer that you want disability income or paid medical leave benefits. Otherwise, they may assume that you only want an unpaid leave.

Identify the administrator of your disability claim. It is *not* going to be your human resources department. If you are applying for Employer Sponsored benefits, the administrator can be an insurance company or a third-party administrator. If you are applying for State Disability, the administrator can also be a State Plan. The State Plan is the default State Disability insurance, usually run by a department of the state government.

Complete the disability claim form (online, PDF, or paper) and submit to the administrator. Ask people to help you if necessary. Don't shy away from help. Remember, you can be resilient and vulnerable. Don't listen to Lord Lizard, you don't have to face the world alone.

The form will ask you for an Onset Date of Disability (i.e., the day your illness began to disable you from work). Don't confuse this with the onset of your *illness*, which can be weeks or even years prior to the Onset Date of Disability. Generally, your Onset Date of Disability is on or right after the Date Last Work (DLW), depending on the rules of the particular insurance you apply for. The Onset Date starts the Waiting Period.

Claims can be denied because of technicalities around the Onset Date. For example, the claimant became disabled during an unauthorized leave, or a large gap exists between the Onset Date and the DLW, or the claim is made after termination. In these cases, the insurer may say the claimant became disabled outside of the coverage period. Different insurers will care about different technicalities; the issue is complex and beyond the scope of this book. If your claim is denied due to the Onset Date, don't give up. Find an attorney to appeal your case.

SEVEN STEPS TO YOUR PAID MEDICAL LEAVE: INTRODUCTION

Ask your doctor to certify your disability claim. Make sure you and your doctor put down the same Onset Date of Disability. Any discrepancies may delay or ruin your claim.

The claim form may ask if your disability is related to work. Some insurers may deny your claim due to a worker's compensation exclusion in the policy. Others may allow the claim but require you to apply for worker's compensation. If you win the worker's compensation claim, the disability insurer will want their money back. Still others won't let you make a claim unless you have already been denied on your worker's compensation claim. Talk to your doctor to clarify the basis of the claim. Did your illness begin before your current job? Is the illness triggered by personal events (divorce, death of parents)? Talk to a worker's compensation attorney if you are confused.

Your employer may need to fill out part of the form. The form may ask your employer to provide a description of your job duties. Make sure the description is correct and updated to reflect your current job.

Review your notes from Step Two on application deadlines. Beware of the appropriate time to submit your claim. Some disability insurances require you to submit the claim after your Onset Date of Disability, while others allow you to submit a claim before the Onset Date. Some insurances, such as California State Disability, won't accept your claim until after your Waiting Period.

On Employer Sponsored claims, I recommend that you hire an ERISA attorney to represent or advise you. Commercial insurers can be quite aggressive in denying and suspending claims.

So far, we have assumed applying for disability income is separate from applying for job and health insurance protections. However, some large employers combine the process, and you only have to apply once for all three protections, probably through the employer's absence management company.

If you are denied disability benefits, don't give up and don't procrastinate. Seek the advice of an attorney and appeal as soon as possible. If you don't know where to find an attorney, call your state bar.

Step Six: Rest, Heal, and Maintain Your Benefits

You have begun your paid medical leave. You are receiving Short-Term Disability income or Paid Family Medical Leave (PFML). Your job and health insurance are protected by state and federal laws. You or your company continue to pay your health insurance.

While the heavy lifting is done, you still need to maintain your claim. Continue medical treatment. Report symptoms and functional limitations to your doctor. The insurer may stop your disability income benefit if you don't. You may need your doctor to recertify your disability from time to time.

Keep in touch with the administrator of your disability benefits. They may ask you for updated medical records and forms. If you don't respond, they may stop your disability income.

Make sure health insurance premiums are paid *on time*.

Be careful with social media. Some insurance companies and third-party administrators monitor their claimants. For example, if your disability claim is based on anxiety in public and your Facebook account shows you happily shopping and partying, the insurer will doubt your claim and stop payments.

Step Seven: Consider Your Future

A paid medical leave is the perfect time to reflect on your job satisfaction and reprioritize your life. You may have been too busy, but now you don't have any excuse. Calendar the last date of your leave. Before your leave ends, explore your options for your career, health, and life. Consult your therapist, doctor, attorney, spirit guide, family, and friends.

Option 1: Go back to the same job

At the end of the three-month leave, you go back to the same job. Sometimes you just need an extended break. You love what you do and are ready to recommit to your job. 恭喜! Congratulations! In that case, confirm with your doctor that you are medically fit to go back to work. Your employer or insurer may need your doctor to certify that you can go back to work.

You can try returning to work part time. Check with your insurer to see if you can go on partial disability. If yes, you can receive both wage and disability income. For example, your Short-Term Disability pays up to 60 percent of your regular income and allows you to earn up to 40 percent of your pre-disability income without affecting your benefit. In this case, you may start working two days a week before transitioning back to full time.

If you need help from your employer to return to work, see if you qualify for "reasonable accommodation" under the American with Disabilities Act (ADA). Accommodations for mental health include flexible work schedule, modified break schedule, quiet area, support animal/person, etc. If your employer denies your request for accommodation, don't quit (which many workers do because they feel demoralized). Consult an employment attorney. They can guide you from behind the scenes or negotiate directly with your employer.

Since you are returning to the same job, your health insurance should remain the same. Your employer should resume paying your insurance premium if they stopped during your leave.

If your illness becomes disabling again, you can claim disability income again. If the claim stems from the same illness, you may bypass the Waiting Period. Consider applying for Long-Term Disability if your illness returns or worsens.

Continue to see your doctor, and document your symptoms and functional limitations in case you need to file for Long-Term Disability.

Keep a tab of how many days of your FMLA you have used. You are entitled to twelve weeks of it every twelve months. If you need to go on disability again and you don't have FMLA days left, request a leave under the employer's policy.

Option 2: Switch jobs

Sometimes your illness is an awakening. It awakens you to the fact that your job sucks. It is hurting your health. Consider switching to a job that is better for your health.

Or you may want to switch to another job that better serves your life's purpose.

Or your job is killing you. That's another good reason to change jobs.

If transitioning to a new career sounds hard, consider using career services, such as your state's Department of Rehabilitation and commercial staffing agencies.

SEVEN STEPS TO YOUR PAID MEDICAL LEAVE: INTRODUCTION

If you have a new employer, then you need to switch health insurance. Your new health insurance will take some time to kick in. While you are waiting for your new health insurance from your new employer, stay on your old health insurance by electing COBRA.

The COBRA administrator will notify you of your eligibility for health insurance continuation. You have sixty days from the date of the notice or the date you would lose coverage (whichever is later) to elect COBRA. But don't wait until the last minute to elect. You have forty-five days from the date of election to pay the first premium.

While you are waiting for your COBRA election to be processed, continue to see your doctor. You don't have to wait until your election is completed to see doctors, as your health insurance is still active during the election process.

If the COBRA administrator does not receive your COBRA election, you will lose your health insurance. So, keep copies of your COBRA election paperwork, and use certified mail. If you can elect online and get a confirmation online, even better.

If your employer has paid health insurance premiums for you during your leave, you may have to pay those back if you don't return to your employer. This may affect your decision of when and how to quit. Some people return to their job for a while before transitioning out (so they don't have to pay their employer back). However, an exception exists under the FMLA. If you cannot return to your job due to a serious illness, you may not have to pay your employer back.

Option 3: Stay on Disability

You don't have to go back to work if you are still sick. Instead, you can stay on your disability income.

At some point, your employer will terminate the employment relationship. Elect your COBRA when you leave your company, just like in Option 2. If your COBRA is too expensive, consider buying an individual health insurance policy, which may be cheaper, especially if you get one through the Affordable Care Act (ACA) and qualify for financial assistance from the federal government.

While COBRA may be more expensive, it may be more convenient, since you (and your dependents) will retain the same insurance you are familiar with. When you switch to an individual health insurance, you may not be able to see the same doctor or get the same drugs. I highly recommend that you get a health insurance broker to help you choose; their commission comes from the health insurance company, not you.

As mentioned above, check if your employer will require you to pay back whatever benefits they may have paid for you during your leave.

If you choose to stay on disability, a key question is *how long your Short-Term Disability income can last.* Here are four scenarios within Option 3:

Scenario 1: If your Short-Term Disability *cannot* last longer (or much longer) than your medical leave, you must apply for Long-Term Disability income immediately. For example, your leave is the standard three months of FMLA, and your STDI also lasts only three months. If you don't apply for Long-Term Disability right away, you risk a gap in income.

SEVEN STEPS TO YOUR PAID MEDICAL LEAVE: INTRODUCTION

After your three months of job protection is over, your employer may terminate you for not returning to work. When your job is gone, so is your group health insurance, so you will need to get new health insurance. One possibility is to continue your health insurance with COBRA. If your dependents are on your health insurance, they can continue with COBRA too. Or you can buy your own individual policies, such as Obamacare.

Example:

> Viktoria and her doctors agreed that she shouldn't work for at least six months. Both her FMLA leave and STDI were for only three months. When she knew she wouldn't return to work when her STDI ended, she applied for LTDI immediately. When she didn't return to work at the end of her FMLA leave, her employer terminated her, and she used COBRA for health insurance. During her FMLA leave, her employer paid part of her health insurance premium. She didn't have to pay this back because her reason for not returning to work was her serious illness.

Scenario 2: If your Short-Term Disability *can* last longer than your leave, you can exhaust your leave, then exhaust your Short-Term Disability, then go back to work. Workers opt for this when they want to take a break longer than their FMLA, but do not want to apply for Long-Term Disability. Here is a typical case: your FMLA leave is three months long and your STDI (or State Disability) lasts up to six months. Instead of returning to your old job when the three months is up, you stay on your Short-Term Disability. When the Short-Term Disability ends, you return to work.

Example:

> Fritz had major depression. He decided to stop working after a couple of suicide attempts. He worked in Hawaii and had up to six months of State Disability and three months of FMLA leave. His employer also provided a Long-Term Disability policy with a six-month Waiting Period. When his FMLA leave ended, he was still too depressed to return to work, so his psychiatrist continued to certify his State Disability. His employer eventually terminated him. After he exhausted his six months of State Disability, he found a new job and returned to work. Altogether, he took half a year off from work to heal his depression. He never claimed Long-Term Disability.

Scenario 3: Not all leaves are limited to three months. Some companies integrate their protected leave policy with their Short-Term Disability benefit. In these cases, as long as you are on the company's Short-Term Disability income, your employment is protected.

Example:

> Nicola worked for a university and was covered under their STDI. The university's STDI lasted up to six months. When she got on the STDI, her job was automatically protected for up to six months by the university's employment policy, regardless of the three-month limitation of FMLA.

Some employers may offer you COBRA after you exhaust your FMLA protection, even if you maintain your employee status. Confirm with your employer on how they will continue your health insurance beyond your FMLA leave.

Scenario 4: The last scenario is when your Short-Term Disability can last longer than your three-month FMLA leave, but you don't

SEVEN STEPS TO YOUR PAID MEDICAL LEAVE: INTRODUCTION 113

return to work at the end of your short-term disability. Instead, you transition onto Long-Term Disability protections: SSDI or LTDI.

Example:

> Yehudi had schizophrenia. He worked in California and was entitled to twelve months of State Disability. However, he and his doctors knew that he wouldn't be able to work for at least a couple of years. That's why he applied for Social Security Disability Insurance (SSDI) right after he stopped working. He wanted to make sure when his State Disability ended, he was already on SSDI. Otherwise, he would be without any income. He did not have any Employer Sponsored disability insurance.

Example:

> Pablo stopped working because of his bipolar disorder. At first, he got on his Employer Sponsored Short-Term Disability Insurance (STDI), which he knew would last for six months. After a couple of months of STDI payments, he decided he should take a year off to rest and heal, so he applied for his Employer Sponsored Long-Term Disability Insurance (LTDI). When his STDI payments ended, he was transitioned onto LTDI payments. His LTDI insurer required him to apply for SSDI because of subrogation. He obliged and was awarded SSDI as well. After twenty-four months of SSDI payments, he got Medicare.

• • •

The process of claiming Long-Term Disability can be complicated. Compared to Short-Term Disability, Long-Term Disability requires more forms to fill out, more follow-ups with doctors, and more scrutiny from the insurer. After all, more money is at stake. While the short-term claims can last a few months or even a year, long-term claims can last many years or even a lifetime. Insurers search for reasons to deny your claim. They search even after initial approval, so that they can discontinue your claim.

The transition from short- to long-term claims is like teenage years. For some people, it is smooth and uneventful. For others, it is traumatic. A common complaint from my clients is: "How come [my aunt, my friend, my neighbor] got approved within months and my case is still pending?" I used to reply, "every case is different." But that didn't ameliorate their pain and suffering. They were running out of money. They felt betrayed by their employers and the disability insurance companies. They were upset that the Social Security kept losing their medical records. They were being evicted. A myriad of misfortunes.

To smooth your transition, I recommend two things:

1. Plan early. Early is when you are still working and considering taking time off for your health. Early is when you and your doctor begin to discuss the possibility of your medical leave. Early is when you just started receiving your Short-Term Disability payments.
2. Hire attorneys for your ERISA and Social Security claims from the get-go. Have them set up your claims for success from the very beginning. There is too much at stake.

Epilogue

If you know you are worthy of love, however useless you may seem to be to the society, even as useless as the running rain, as American monk Thomas Merton put it, then you may finally allow yourself to rest and heal. Give up those "Can I" questions. Let go of the temptation to suffer. Release yourself from your own prison. So long, Lord Lizard.

I said this before, and I will say it again. What do you want to do with your life? Who is it that you really love? What haven't you done that you regret most? *Who are you?* Perhaps in your busy life, you haven't had the chance to consider any of these questions. Like it or not, now is your chance—a bittersweet 恭喜.

Be brave; it takes guts to declare: I have a serious illness. I need a medical leave. I am going to apply for benefits. I am going to put my finances in order. I am going to rest and heal. I am going to reconnect with the people and things I love the most.

So goodbye for now. If this book brings you joy and hope, more confidence in directing your own affairs, and discernment in your choices around taking time off for your mental health, then I have done my job.

Glossary

Adjudicator A person or team that determines whether you are "disabled" for the purposes of disability insurance. They work for the insurer, which can be an insurance company or government department.

Administrator A commercial company or government department that processes, pays, approves, or denies disability claims. Some commercial administrators also process medical leave requests and are known as an "absence management company."

Affordable Care Act (ACA) A federal law that allows more people to access health insurance. Under this law, many people can access insurance without being poor, elderly, disabled, or part of an employment group. Some people call it Obamacare.

American with Disabilities Act (ADA) A federal law that helps people with physical or mental illness obtain and maintain employment. Under the law, employers must provide "reasonable accommodation" to the employees.

Commercial Insurance Insurance from the private industry, such as UNUM and Hartford. Contrast with Public Insurance.

Consolidated Omnibus Budget Reconciliation Act (COBRA) This federal law allows you and your dependents to continue your Employer Sponsored health insurance after you leave your job. You can continue it for up to eighteen months.

Disability Insurance A type of insurance that replaces lost income due to disability.

Employer Sponsored Group benefits provided through your employer, such as disability insurance and health insurance. See Group Insurance.

Employer Sponsored Long-Term Disability Insurance (LTDI) A type of disability insurance that employees get through their employer. It usually pays as long as the claimant is disabled.

Employer Sponsored Short-Term Disability Insurance (STDI) A type of disability insurance that employees get through their employer. It usually pays up to six months of disability benefits.

Employment Attorney Attorneys who focus on employment law issues between the employer and the employee, such as wage, medical leave, and reasonable workplace accommodation.

ERISA Attorney Attorneys who focus on employee benefits regulated by the Employee Retirement Income Security Act of 1974 (ERISA). They represent clients on LTDI and STDI claims.

Family Medical Leave Act (FMLA) A federal law that provides up to twelve weeks of medical leave every twelve months. During the FMLA leave, your job and health insurance are protected. It does not provide income benefits.

GLOSSARY

Function Report A set of questions for the claimant to answer about his symptoms and function limitations. Insurer uses it to determine whether the claimant is disabled.

Functional Limitation The way your illness limits your activities of work and daily living.

Group Insurance Insurance that is purchased through a group, such as employment or professional association. All Employer Sponsored insurances are Group Insurances. Contrast with Individual Insurance.

Health Insurance Portability and Accountability Act (HIPAA) A federal law that provides privacy and other rights to patients.

Individual Insurance Insurance that is purchased directly from the insurer and not through a group, like employment or professional associations. Some people call it "private" insurance. Contrast with Group Insurance.

Insurer An entity that provides disability insurance coverage. It can be public or commercial. Public insurers are government programs such as Social Security and State Plan. Commercial insurers are usually insurance companies such as UNUM, Hartford. The largest insurer in the United States is, by far, the Social Security Administration (SSA).

Long-Term Disability (1) A longer period away from work to rest and heal, usually at least six months. (2) Long-Term Disability benefits, such as SSDI and LTDI.

Onset Date of Disability The beginning date of a disability claim. It starts the Waiting Period for disability benefits.

Paid Family Medical Leave (PFML) State laws that provide income when the worker is seriously ill. Some also provide job and health insurance protections. It is available in the District of

Columbia, Connecticut, Washington State, Massachusetts, and, in 2023, Oregon.

Private Insurance A term that can mean Individual Insurance (as opposed to Group Insurance) or Commercial Insurance (as opposed to Public Insurance). To avoid confusion, I don't use the term in this book.

Public Insurance Any disability insurance that is required by law, such as Social Security Disability Insurance and the various State Disability and Paid Family Medical Leave programs. Contrast with Commercial Insurance.

Six Places The six jurisdictions that require State Disability: California, Hawaii, New York, New Jersey, Rhode Island, and Puerto Rico.

State Disability A type of Short-Term Disability Insurance mandated by state law in California, Hawaii, New York, New Jersey, Rhode Island, and Puerto Rico. Most people who have State Disability have the State Plan. Others may have commercial policies as substitute.

State Plan State Disability insurance run by a state government agency. Most people who have State Disability have the State Plan. Others may have commercial policies as a substitute.

Social Security Attorney Attorneys who focus on Social Security disability benefits, such as SSDI and SSI.

Social Security Disability Income (SSDI) A type of disability insurance administered by the Social Security Administration (SSA). It covers most US workers and is linked with Medicare.

Supplemental Security Income (SSI) A federal benefit that provides income to the elderly and disabled. Only people with limited resources and income qualify. It is linked with Medicaid in many states.

Short-Term Disability   (1) A short period away from work to rest and heal, usually three to six months. (2) Short-Term Disability benefits, such as State Disability or Employer Sponsored Short-Term Disability Insurance (STDI).

Symptom   Your experience of your illness.

Triangle of Definition   This diagram illustrates the model definition of "disability" within the world of disability income.

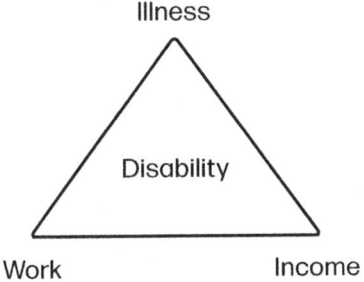

Triangle of Protections   This diagram reminds us of what we should protect when we take a paid medical leave.

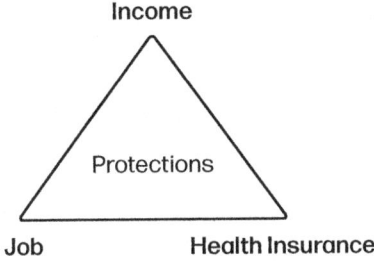

Triangle of Social Security Disability This diagram shows how the Social Security Administration defines "disability."

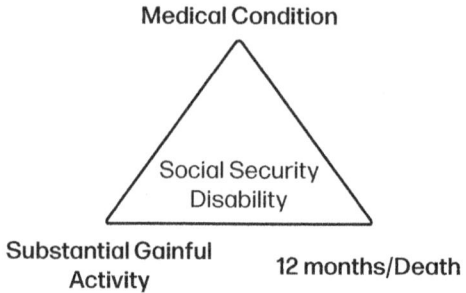

Triangle of Understanding This diagram shows how information travels from you to the Adjudicator.

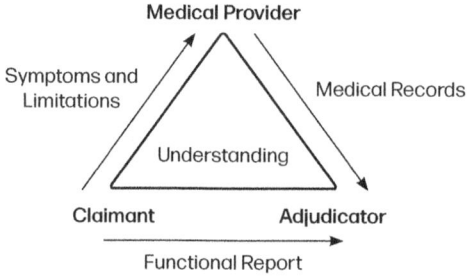

Waiting Period The period the claimant must wait before he can *apply* or *receive* disability benefits. Sometimes it means both. For example, California State Disability requires the claimant to wait seven days of disability before he can apply *and* those seven days are not payable (i.e., no retroactive benefit for those seven days of disability). It is sometimes called the elimination period in Employer Sponsored disability policies.

恭喜 The phrase means *congratulations* in Cantonese, pronounced gong hei.

Acknowledgments

I would like to thank my editor Leslie Schwartz, as well as my beta readers Alison Mastrangelo, Lisa Koshkarian, Jonathan and Pamela Hiller, Nina Wasow, Paul Fishman, Eugene Stuart, Charles Mujie, Scott Kalkin, and Evan Xu.

About Me

I began my legal career as a public interest attorney in 2003. I worked at a nonprofit called Positive Resource Center (PRC) where I represented low-income folks on their disability claims and health insurance. The best part of my job was the clients. We developed trust and I learned what it means to help people without attachment. We celebrated successes and fought the odds (and the odds against the poor are never good).

In 2009, I became the legal director of PRC. My new job was to train new attorneys and supervise the legal team. There was a lot of administrative work too. Over the years, I have represented and supervised thousands of disability claims, about half of them mental health related.

From 2014 to 2019, the last few years of my tenure at PRC, I collaborated with governments and foundations to implement new social services. I designed social programs to help people secure housing, access income, and exercise their rights under the Affordable Care Act. In 2020, I began my solo law practice.

I was born in Hong Kong and am a native Cantonese speaker. I graduated from UC Hastings College of the Law in 2002 and UC Berkeley in 1997. My bachelor's degree was in anthropology.

Here is a picture of me with a puppy.

Made in the USA
Las Vegas, NV
07 July 2023

74264768R00077